CW01623665

A Liturgy of Sorrow

A Liturgy of Sorrow

SERVICES OF PENANCE
FOR COMMUNAL CELEBRATION

Edited by
DAVID KONSTANT

Contributors
Jim Brand, Michael Cockett,
John Coghlan, David Konstant,
Kevin Nichols, Leo Pyle,
Sylvia Ross, Winifred Wilson

MAYHEW-McCRIMMON
Great Wakering

First published in Great Britain in 1975 by
MAYHEW-McCRIMMON LTD
10-12 High Street
Great Wakering Essex

ISBN 0-85597-092-8

Nihil obstat — Brian O'Higgins
Imprimatur — C. D. Creede, Vic.Gen
Brentwood Nov. 13 1975

Acknowledgements

The scripture texts are taken from the Jerusalem Bible Version of the Scriptures, copyrighted © in 1966, 1967 and 1968 by Darton, Longman and Todd Ltd., and Doubleday and Co. Inc., and used by permission.
The version of the Psalms is that translated from the Hebrew by the Grail, copyright © 1963, the Grail (England) and published by William Collins and Sons Ltd. in The Psalms: A New Translation. Used by permission.
English translation of the Rite of Penance copyright © 1975, International Committee on English in the Liturgy, Inc. All rights reserved.

Printed by Mayhew-McCrimmon Ltd

Contents

Preface

These Services of Penance are offered for all those who may have a hand in the preparation of such services – the parish clergy, school chaplains, religious, teachers, liturgical committees. Individuals also may be helped by the prayers, readings and reflections contained in the book, to come to a deeper understanding and experience of God's forgiving love.

Although the revised form of penance has not yet been officially introduced, it is hoped that these Services of Penance may play a part in the gradual initiation of priests and laity into the new rite of the sacrament.

The following services have been based on the sample texts prepared by the Congregation for Divine Worship (the ICEL translation) and, along with the *Form of Examination of Conscience* on page 163, are included by permission; 2, 3, 8, 12, 13, 14, 15, 19, 34.

There are two numberings for most of the psalms: the first number follows that used in translations from the Greek or Latin, the second number in brackets follows the Hebrew numbering.

The following hymn and song books are referred to:

FH: 20th Century Folk Hymnal, volumes 1 & 2 (Mayhew-McCrimmon)

PTL: Praise the Lord (New Revised Edition) (Geoffrey Chapman)

BHP: Biblical Hymns and Psalms, Deiss (Geoffrey Chapman)

NHS: New Hymns for All Seasons, Quinn (Geoffrey Chapman)

HYC: Hymns for Young Christians, Wilson (Geoffrey Chapman)

PC: 24 Psalms and a Canticle (Grail)

David Konstant

Westminster Religious
Education Centre

October, 1975

Introduction

We profess 'one Lord, one faith, and one baptism,' and we belong to one another as members of one body – the body of Christ. This belonging makes what we do deeply significant, and gives us added responsibility for our actions. Our failures weaken the whole community; our successes strengthen the whole community; our growth is made possible through the whole community. In a sense, by being Christians we cease to be private persons; whatever we do or fail to do it is as these Christians, these members of Christ's body, that we act or fail to act in this way.

One of the rich understandings of today is an increased awareness of the Church as a community: the Church is Christ, and we are the Church. At a time when the individual is often swamped by the tide of officialdom, by the impersonality of the assembly-line, and by the size of so many institutions, it can be enormously encouraging to realise that we are deeply bound up with each other as Christians.

Dependence on each other can, of course, be enslaving – the relationship between the serf and his feudal lord, or even between the employee and his employer, used to be of this sort. But the person who has learnt how to live as a Christian finds in his dependence on others a genuine freedom. In his search for freedom someone may first of all try to be completely independent, and may imagine that the only person he can really trust is himself; then he discovers that self-reliance does not answer his needs. He may even learn that the last person in the world he can trust is himself. This discovery – that he has not got to rely on himself for everything – is a wonderfully liberating truth, and opens up new horizons and possibilities. He is able to live more confidently; he is able to achieve more; he is given new strength; he finds in himself unexpected powers; he is able to help others in need. Like the early Christians who 'remained faithful to the teaching of the apostles, to the brotherhood, to the breaking of the bread, and to the prayers,' he finds that he belongs to a living body whose head is Christ. Through this belonging comes both his own growth and his chance to serve others. Community living within the Church provides him with the opportunity to use his gifts to the full, and to be supported where he is weakest.

One of the results of the greater appreciation of the community nature of the Church is the attendant realisation that there is a value, and indeed a necessity, for us to express our sorrow for sin and our need for forgiveness, together as a group. We do this in any case whenever we celebrate Mass, which begins with a short service of penance. The Church is now encouraging us to celebrate occasionally a longer and more comprehensive service of penance, especially when we are preparing for Christ's coming (Advent) and for his resurrection (Lent).

The purpose of a service of penance is to help us arrive at a deeper sorrow for sin; to give us a sharper sense of the damage that sin does to the whole community; to make us aware of the support we can be to each other; to help us develop a more sensitive conscience; and to prepare us for a fruitful celebration of the sacrament of penance. A service of penance may be led by anyone, and so may be particularly helpful in those parts of the Church where there are few priests available. Sometimes a service of penance may be celebrated on its own (with or without a priest), on other occasions it may be followed by the opportunity for individual confession and absolution, and on those occasions permitted by the Church it may be concluded by a general absolution.

The suggested pattern of a service of penance is the same as for individual celebration of the sacrament of penance. There is a greeting, an explanation of the service, followed by an invitation to prayer. There is then a liturgy of the word: one or more scriptural readings, along, perhaps, with other appropriate readings; and a homily which develops the theme of the readings. This is followed by an examination of conscience, if possible based on the readings, and the service concludes with a joint act of repentance, followed by the Our Father and a blessing. The object is to provide a framework through which the group is enabled to reflect on its way of living in the light of the gospel – so there need be nothing rigid about the pattern.

There follow a few practical suggestions and comments about the organisation of services of penance.

PREPARATION

Although this book contains a number of worked out services they are not meant to be used just as they stand. Their purpose is to encourage groups to prepare services for themselves, using the printed examples as stimuli for fresh ideas. This is particularly the case with the examination of conscience and act of repentance which should always be prepared by at least some members of the group, since they should be specific to the needs of those who are celebrating. A celebration of this sort is probably going to be a relatively rare event for any one group (say three or four times a year) and plenty of time should be allowed for its preparation.

OCCASION

There are no hard and fast rules. It is clear that Advent and Lent are two very suitable occasions for services of penance – likewise Whitsuntide is an appropriate time since at this feast we celebrate our confirmation as Christians. Other occasions would include retreats, vigils, days of recollection, parish missions, pilgrimages, anniversaries; in short, any occasion which lends itself to reflection on our need for continual conversion.

PARTICIPATION

This is a particularly important element of the celebration because all of us need to see that we are personally involved. It is something we are taking a full part in, and not something being done on our behalf. Just as we contribute to the sin of the world, so also are we healed by sharing in a common act of sorrow and repentance. It is helpful if the service is constructed so that periods of listening are interspersed with more general responses – singing, bidding prayers, short litanies and so on. Also, as many different members of the group as possible may be invited to do the readings, to conduct the examination of conscience, and to lead everyone in an act of repentance.

SIZE OF THE GROUP

This will depend entirely on the circumstances. A group of several thousand on pilgrimage may take part in as helpful and as prayerful a service of penance as will be celebrated by a small group of a dozen people in a private house. We need not look for an exact pattern. The important thing is that a group of Christians want to come together to celebrate their sorrow for sin and their joy in belonging to Christ and to each other.

SYMBOLISM

We communicate with each other in ways other than words, and it is valuable for us in our celebrations to use whatever media are available. An examination of conscience, for instance, could be conducted with the help of a number of pictures, accompanied with a minimum of commentary. Quiet music can be a suitable background for meditative reflection. A dignified mime can deepen our understanding of the spoken word. Candles are richly symbolic of Christ, the light of the world; water is a sign of our baptism. Whatever is going to be helpful as a means to knowing ourselves, expressing our sorrow, and affirming our following of Christ will be proper to our celebration.

EXAMINATION OF CONSCIENCE

This is the response of the group to the word of God. We ask ourselves: 'In the light of the gospel we have listened to, how should we live?' Such a question will encourage the development of an examination of conscience with a positive direction; in other words, the examination will throw light on what we should be doing, and not merely on what we have done wrong. The act of repentance then becomes both an expression of sorrow, and a prayer of hope and of amendment.

SILENCE

This is an essential feature of a service of penance. We need time to pray quietly, to reflect on the word of God, and to think about our way of life in the light of the gospel. Everything should be calm and unhurried, inviting those present to discover peace of heart. The leader should be thoughtful in the way he conducts the service, and should avoid any tendency to act mechanically. In the examination of conscience and the act of repentance enough time should be allowed to let the ideas take root. There need be no anxious looking at watches. The service should be planned to begin on time and to finish when it is ended. Prayer is easier when we are not rushed. Let us remember the prayer of the psalmist: 'Be still, and know that I am God.' (Psalm 45(46).10).

The Following of Christ

(for adult groups, on Ash Wednesday)

ENTRANCE SONG

'Lord, Jesus Christ' FH Vol. 1, no.100

GREETING

May the prayer of Christ, his freedom and his love be with you all.

INTRODUCTION

We have been offered forty days of spiritual training to renew ourselves for Easter. At the Easter Vigil we will be able to confirm our promises and our commitment to Christ. The Church emphasises three ways of imitating Jesus: prayer, fasting and almsgiving. To pray is to allow Jesus to speak to us; it is to listen. To fast is to be in training and alert; to be conscious, awake and sensitive. To give alms is to show love by action; to see the person in need and to respond; to be a friend. We shall be listening to three readings about these ways of imitating Christ; each reading will be followed by a chance to examine the ways we have used or misused our gifts.

PRAYER

Father,
you have given us this holy season of Lent
to remind us that love that drifts grows cool.
Keep us awake and active
so that we may become
more responsible sons and daughters.
Give us the courage to let go of false security
so that we may discover what leads to real joy.
We make our prayer through Christ our Lord.

℟. Amen.

Pause for silent prayer

Father,
we have asked you to fulfil our needs.
Help us to grasp the opportunities you give us,
and to listen to you as you speak to us in prayer.
Give us the courage to pray unceasingly,
the stamina to choose always what is better,
and a warm heart that knows our neighbour
and is careless in giving.

℟. Amen.

FIRST READING

St Paul prayed unceasingly for himself and the world. He thanked God for all his great works. He prayed that Christians would learn perfect wisdom, and like Christ reach a perfect understanding of the Father's will, shown in their lives. He prayed that they would never give in; that they would always seek freedom and forgiveness, and that they would be able to bear anything.

Colossians 1.3-14

ACT OF REPENTANCE

We have taken you for granted: Lord, have mercy.

℟. Lord, have mercy.

We have given you only lip-service: Lord, have mercy. ℟.

We talk much and seldom listen to you: Lord, have mercy. ℟.

We spend hours earning and spending money, and leave so little time for you to speak to us: Lord, have mercy. ℟.

We do not trust you to do what you like with us: Lord, have mercy. ℟.

We find it hard to believe that you love us as we are: Lord, have mercy. ℟.

We feel awkward if we are silent before you: Lord, have mercy. ℟.

We ask you for many things and seldom thank you: Lord, have mercy. ℟.

We have chosen to remain ignorant of your ways: Lord, have mercy. ℟.

We have forgotten that you speak to us through the wonders of nature: Lord, have mercy. ℟.

We fail to see you coming to us in every man: Lord, have mercy. ℟

Canticle:

℟. To him be highest glory and praise for ever.

Daniel 3.57-88, 56

SECOND READING

St Paul had a rule of life. Athletes must keep off the carbohydrates. The pianist must practise hours a day. Sons of God must not make food or riches their gods. They must fill their minds with what is true, honourable, good and pure. This will lead to true joy. Discipline, mortification and fasting are to help us to live in joy.

Philippians 3.17-4.9

ACT OF REPENTANCE

For our soft living: Christ, have mercy.

℟. Christ, have mercy.

If we have amassed the goods and riches of the world: Christ, have mercy. ℟.

For our idleness and sloth: Christ, have mercy. ℟.

When we choose the easy path: Christ, have mercy. ℟.

For refusing to grow in wisdom and maturity: Christ, have mercy. ℟.

If we have let ourselves be imprisoned by circumstances and by the false values of society: Christ, have mercy. ℟.

For our fear of being laughed at because of our standards: Christ, have mercy. ℟.

When we feel we have to keep up with our neighbours in all things: Christ, have mercy. ℟.

If we have undermined the values of others: Christ, have mercy. ℟.

For thinking that mortification and self-denial lead to joylessness: Christ, have mercy. ℟.

For letting everyone know about our achievements: Christ, have mercy. ℟.

For greed and immoderation in food and drink: Christ, have mercy. ℟.

For wasting the earth's resources: Christ, have mercy. ℟.

When we fail to enjoy what we have, because we are bothered about what we are missing: Christ, have mercy. ℟.

Let us join together now in the prayer through which all men seek forgiveness from their Father and from their fellow men.

Our Father . . .

THIRD READING

A good turn, a friendly act, a gesture of love. These take us away from sin.

Luke 7.36-50

ACT OF REPENTANCE

We do not show great love: Lord, have mercy.

℟. Lord, have mercy.

We place limits on our love: Lord, have mercy. ℟.

We are miserly with our treasures: Lord, have mercy. ℟.

We take no interest in the poor of our neighbourhood and in the hungry of the world: Lord, have mercy. ℟.

We take too much care of our own belongings: Lord, have mercy. ℟.

We are blind to the stranger: Lord, have mercy. ℟.

We turn a deaf ear to the person in need: Lord, have mercy. ℟.

We count the cost of our love: Lord, have mercy. ℟.

When we give, we expect much in return: Lord, have mercy. ℟.

We are quick to receive and slow to give: Lord, have mercy. ℟.

We are jealous of our time: Lord, have mercy. ℟.

We are afraid to teach each other our skills: Lord, have mercy. ℟.

We are contemptuous of the poor, the handicapped, and the stupid: Lord, have mercy. ℟.

We honour men for their success and riches: Lord, have mercy. ℟.

We fail to accept persons as sons of God: Lord, have mercy. ℟.

PRAYER FOR FORGIVENESS

Father,
you change us through your word
which calls us to follow your Son.
Help us to be generous in prayer this Lent.
Give us the insight and courage
to live as men and women committed to your will.
Especially give us your generous love for all men
so that through the wounds we will receive
we may learn that the cross is a fair price
for loving and living without limit.
We make our prayer through your Son, Jesus Christ.

℟. Amen.

CONCLUDING SONG

'God's Spirit is in my heart' FH Vol. 1, no.57

A Second Baptism

(for adult groups, to prepare for the Easter Vigil)

ENTRANCE SONG

'All you who seek a comfort sure' PTL, no.176

GREETING

Come to the Lord with faith and confidence, for his love for us is strong, and he is faithful for ever.

INTRODUCTION

St Paul likens baptism to a death and resurrection. The sinner dies to his old ways and rises as a new man, full of grace and truth. The dark waters into which the baptised was plunged were like the tomb in which Christ's body was laid; and the new life of the one who rises from the waters of baptism is to be like Christ's new risen life. Unfortunately, as we well know, we do not live up to our baptismal promise, so each year at the Easter Vigil we have the chance to renew this promise. But before we sincerely make ourselves new again we need a second baptism – the baptism of penance and conversion. We are here now to reflect on what we are called to be as baptised Christians, and to ask forgiveness for our sins.

PRAYER

My brothers and sisters, we have neglected the gifts of our baptism and fallen into sin. Let us ask God to renew his grace within us as we turn to him in repentance.

Bow your heads before God.

Pause for silent prayer

Raise your hearts to God.

Lord Jesus,
you redeemed us by your passion
and raised us to new life in baptism.
Protect us with your unchanging love
and share with us the joy of your resurrection,
for you live and reign for ever and ever.

℟. Amen.

FIRST READING

The pilgrim people led by Moses to their promised land suffered innumerable hardships, and made many mistakes. They slid away from God and turned to the worship of idols; they put God to the test with their behaviour. But God never deserted or forgot them. Whatever our trials we must know that God does not let us be tried beyond our strength.

1 Corinthians 10.1-13

Pause for reflection

Psalm 105(106).6-10,13-14,19-22

℟. Lord, remember us,
for the love you bear your people.

GOSPEL READING

Falling down is not the worst fault, but refusing to be picked up, and turning away from God's forgiving love. The story of the lost sheep reminds us that no one is ever forgotten by God, and that everyone will always find a welcome in his home.
Luke 15.4-7

HOMILY OUTLINE

* The need to fulfil the grace of baptism by living faithfully the Gospel of Christ (1 Corinthians 10.1-13).

* The seriousness of sin committed after baptism (see Hebrews 6.4-8).

* The unlimited mercy of our God and Father who continually welcomes those who turn back to him after having sinned (see Luke 15).

* Easter as the feast when the Church rejoiced over the Christian initiation of catechumens and the reconciliation of penitents.

EXAMINATION OF CONSCIENCE

A sample examination of conscience prepared by the Congregation for Divine Worship is given on page 163. Other examinations will be found throughout the book. On this occasion it is good to examine ourselves in the light of our baptismal promises.
When we were baptised, we promised to reject sin, so as to live in the freedom of God's children.

Have we allowed ourselves to become enslaved to anything which makes us less than we are called to be? What is our attitude to comfort, to food and drink, to money and property? Do we accept the guidance of law as the way to freedom? Do we enslave other people by putting wrong pressures on them, by discouraging them, by refusing to forgive, by being too demanding, by being over-protective, by keeping them in ignorance, by frightening them, by denying them proper food, drink, clothing, or housing?

When we were baptised, we promised to reject the glamour of evil, and to refuse to be mastered by sin.

Have we been fooled by the easy attractiveness of permissiveness? Have our values become those of the world? Have our consciences become lax? What is the rule of our lives – the gospel, or selfish convenience? Do we serve God or Mammon? Do we respect ourselves and others? Are we willing to be mastered by God's Spirit?

When we were baptised, we promised to reject Satan, father of sin and prince of darkness.

Do we follow the path of truth, honesty, openness, and sincerity? Or do we walk in the dark ways of deceit, fraud, bigotry, and hypocrisy? Do we listen to God in prayer? Do we see God in our fellow men and in the world we live in? Do we try to grow in knowledge and understanding of God? Do we accept our need for God and our dependence on him, or do we try to make our way without him? What do we reject in our lives and what do we accept?

With these reflections in mind, let us now renew our baptismal promises.

Do you reject sin, so as to live in the freedom of God's children?

℟. I do.

Do you reject the glamour of evil, and refuse to be mastered by sin?

℟. I do.

Do you reject Satan, father of sin and prince of darkness?

℟. I do.

ACT OF REPENTANCE

My brothers and sisters, the hour of God's favour draws near, the day of his mercy and of our salvation, when death was destroyed and eternal life began. This is the season for planting new vines in God's vineyard, the time for pruning the vines to ensure a richer harvest.

We all acknowledge that we are sinners. We are moved to penance, encouraged by the example and prayers of our brothers and sisters. We admit our guilt and say: 'Lord, I acknowledge my sins; my offences are always before me. Turn away your face, Lord, from my sins, and blot out all my wrong-doing. Give me back the joy of your salvation and give me a new and steadfast spirit.'

We are sorry for having offended God by our sins. May he be merciful and hear us as we ask to be restored to his friendship and numbered among the living who share the joy of Christ's risen life.

Then the priest sprinkles the people with holy water, while all say:

> Cleanse us, Lord, from all our sins;
> Wash us, and we shall be whiter than snow.

Lord our God,
you created us in love
and redeemed us in mercy.
While we were exiled from heaven
by the jealousy of the evil one,
you gave us your only Son,
who shed his blood to save us.
Send now your Holy Spirit
to breathe new life into your children,
for you do not want us to die
but to live for you alone.
You do not abandon those who abandon you;
correct us as a Father
and restore us to your family.

Lord,
your sons and daughters stand before you
in humility and trust.
Look with compassion on us
as we confess our sins.
Heal our wounds;
stretch out a hand of pity
to save us and raise us up.
Keep us free from harm
as members of Christ's body,
as sheep of your flock,

as children of your family.
Do not allow the enemy
to triumph over us
or death to claim us for ever,
for you raised us to new life in baptism.

Hear, Lord, the prayers we offer from contrite hearts.
Have pity on us as we acknowledge our sins.
Lead us back to the way of holiness.
Protect us now and always
from the wounds of sin.
May we ever keep safe in all its fulness
the gift your love once gave us
and your mercy now restores.

We ask this through our Lord Jesus Christ, your Son,
who lives and reigns with you and the Holy Spirit,
one God for ever and ever.

℟. Amen

BLESSING AND DISMISSAL

As we have died to sin in baptism,
so may we all rise with Christ
to a new life of peace, justice and holiness.
And may the blessing of almighty God,
the Father, Son and Holy Spirit,
be with you now and always.

℟. Amen.

Go in the peace of Christ.

℟. Thanks be to God.

CONCLUDING SONG

'O praise ye the Lord!' PTL no.4

That the World may be Saved

(for parish groups, during Lent)

ENTRANCE SONG

'O Lord, my God' FH Vol.2, no.27

GREETING

May our minds and hearts be renewed, so that we can put on a new self, in the goodness and holiness of truth.

INTRODUCTION

We cannot fail to realise how much we depend on each other. Water, gas, electricity, telephones, the shops round the corner, buses and trains, dustcarts and so on – all these depend on people. More than that we need each other as persons. Friendship and companionship are qualities of living that we want more than anything else. But people do not behave in a friendly or peaceable way always, which is why the world is in such a mess. Our sins are part of this mess; when we sin we help to make the world a worse place to live in for everyone else. We are now being invited to help clear up the mess, so that as a family we can make the world a better place to live in. Our prayer together now is that through our sorrow and conversion others may be led to know, love and serve God.

PRAYER

My brothers and sisters, let us pray that by penance we may be united with Christ, who was crucified for our sins, and so share with all mankind in his resurrection.

Pause for silent prayer

Lord, our God and Father,
through the passion of your Son
you gave us new life.
By our practice of penance
make us one with him in his dying
so that we and all mankind
may be one with him

in his resurrection.

We ask this through Christ our Lord.

℟. Amen.

FIRST READING

It is always the innocent who suffer as the result of someone else's fault. Whether at the time we think of it or not, whenever we in any way fall short of what we could be, we harm others. This reading from Isaiah is a deeply moving picture of the suffering of the good man; it is a picture true of all people trampled on by sin, and most true of Jesus Christ, who took on himself the sins of the whole world.

Isaiah 53.1-7,10-12

Pause for reflection

The suffering servant of God wins salvation for everyone.
Where sin abounded, grace now abounds even more.

Psalm 21(22).2-3,7-9,18-28

℟. All the peoples of the earth shall remember,
and return to the Lord.

SECOND READING

St Peter comments on Isaiah's prophecy, and reminds us that Christ is our shepherd and guardian.

1 Peter 2.19-24

Pause for reflection

GOSPEL READING

Christ took on the sins of the world by being the slave to all. We become his followers and help to ransom the world if we learn to be the least, and to serve the poorest in the kingdom. When we accept baptism and the eucharist we accept a share in the sufferings of Christ; without such a share we cannot hope to share his glory.

Mark 10.32-45

HOMILY OUTLINE

* By sin we offend God and also Christ's body, the Church, whose members we became in baptism.

* Sin is a failure of love for Christ who in the paschal mystery

showed his love for us to the end.

* The way we affect each other when we do good or choose evil.

* The mystery of vicarious satisfaction by which Christ bore the burden of our sins, so that by his wounds we would be healed (see Isaiah 53, 1 Peter 2.24).

* The social and ecclesial dimension of penance by which individual Christians share in the work of converting the whole community.

* The celebration of Easter as the feast of the Christian community which is renewing itself by the conversion or repentance of each member, so that the Church may become a clearer sign of salvation in the world.

EXAMINATION OF CONSCIENCE

A sample examination of conscience prepared by the Congregation for Divine Worship is given on page 163. Other examinations will be found throughout the book.

ACT OF REPENTANCE

Let us confess our sins together:

I confess to almighty God, . . .

As a sign of our conversion and sorrow, and of our love of others there may be some practical gesture we can make which will help others to celebrate the feast of Easter with joy. *The celebrant may suggest what could be done, for example, visiting the sick, a community work of service, a collection for the Third World.*

Let us join together in the prayer in which we acknowledge God as our Father, and in which we seek forgiveness from him and from each other.

Our Father . . .

Deliver us, Father, from every evil
as we unite ourselves through penance
with the saving passion of your Son.
Grant us a share
in the joy of the resurrection of Jesus
who is Lord for ever and ever.

℟. Amen.

Depending on circumstances, the general confession may be followed by a form of devotion such as adoration of the cross or the way of the cross, according to local custom and the wishes of the people.

BLESSING AND DISMISSAL

May the passion of our Lord Jesus Christ,
the intercession of the blessed virgin Mary,
and of all the saints,
whatever good you do, and suffering you endure,
heal your sins,
help you to grow in holiness,
and reward you with eternal life.

And may almighty God bless you,
the Father, the Son and the Holy Spirit.

℟. Amen.

Go in peace, to love and serve the Lord.

℟. Thanks be to God.

CONCLUDING SONG

'Christ be beside me' FH Vol.2, no.13

Open to the Spirit

(for parish groups, in preparation for Pentecost)

ENTRANCE SONG

'Light up the fire' FH Vol.2, no.1

GREETING

May our hearts be open to the power and love of the Spirit.

INTRODUCTION

The Holy Spirit is the presence of Jesus in us, in the community of the Church, and in the world. He is no longer limited by time and space. Having passed through death, he lives for ever with the Father. Through the Spirit he penetrates the whole of creation and especially the inmost being of man. He is the dynamic power within the Church, urging it forward, making it aware of the signs of the times, bringing about necessary change to enable the gospel to be preached to modern man. It is he who inspires us to action, raising up apostles and prophets. He is the love of God, offering itself to the world. For each of us, too, he is power and love, rousing us from sluggishness and selfishness, inviting us to friendship with God, and to fuller and more joyful life. He calls us to open our hearts.

PRAYER

Spirit of God, help us during this time of shared reflection and prayer to open up the depths of our being to your light and love.

Pause for silent prayer

God our Father,
thank you for the gift of the Spirit
through whom we experience your loving care,
and through whom we are made like Jesus Christ, your Son.

℟. Amen.

FIRST READING

In his letter to the Galatians, St Paul describes the effect of the Spirit in our lives.

Galatians 5.22-26

Pause for reflection

Psalm 138(139).1,3,4,6,12

℟. Your hand is ever upon me,
you lead me and hold me fast.

SECOND READING

Jesus gives God's Spirit to the world. Immediately after his redemptive death the Spirit flowed out from him. Many examples of the outpouring of the Spirit are recorded in the early Church. But great emphasis was placed on the first, which took place fifty days after Easter, on the day on which the giving of the Law to Moses was annually celebrated. On this occasion, the feast of Pentecost, this gift of the new covenant was first bestowed very palpably on the apostles and their friends.

Acts 2.1-6

Pause for reflection

Song: 'Grant to us, O Lord, a heart renewed' BHP, page 38.

GOSPEL READING

Jesus breathes his life, his Spirit, into the apostles after the resurrection.

John 20.19-23

HOMILY OUTLINE

* What the apostles actually saw or heard at Pentecost does not really matter. What is described dramatically is an experience through which they became transformed men, filled with God's Spirit, alive with Jesus's own life.

* They could now continue Christ's work.

* Pentecost was a day of new things, new life, new values, a new relationship with Jesus.

* This applies to us.

* Special gifts of the Spirit (tongues, prophesying, healings, and so on) are less in evidence today than in the early Church, but they do still occur.

* The present fruits of the Spirit are more ordinary, fitting in everywhere – home, school, work. Note 1 Corinthians 13 for the 'greatest of these.'

EXAMINATION OF CONSCIENCE

How aware are we of the presence of the Spirit within us, ready to animate us and give meaning to our lives?

Do we recognise the fruits of the Spirit in others and respond to them?

Do we believe that the Spirit is active in the present ferment in the Church?

Do we block the action of the Spirit through fear or prejudice?

If we are to be sensitive and responsive to the Spirit, we must pray. Does prayer have a place in our lives?

Can we be quiet, relaxed and receptive in the presence of the Spirit?

ACT OF REPENTANCE

For our indifference to the Spirit: forgive us, Lord

℟. Forgive us, Lord.

For the absence of the signs of the Spirit in our lives: forgive us, Lord. ℟.

For blocking the work of the Spirit in ourselves, in others, and in the community: forgive us, Lord. ℟.

For our failure to call on and use the power of the Spirit: forgive us, Lord. ℟.

For the absence of prayer in our lives: forgive us, Lord. ℟.

For our want of faith, hope and love: forgive us, Lord. ℟.

Father,
may we be made whole
and filled by grace with your Spirit

℟. Amen.

FINAL PRAYER AND BLESSING

God our Father,
through the Holy Spirit who is in us,
help us to work for a true renewal

of the Christian community and of ourselves.
May our striving for God's kingdom not fail through selfishness or fear;
may the universe be alive with the Spirit,
and may our own homes be pledges of a world redeemed.

℟. Amen.

CONCLUDING SONG

'We are one in the Spirit' FH Vol.1, no.46

The Power of the Spirit

(for parish groups, in preparation for Pentecost)

ENTRANCE SONG

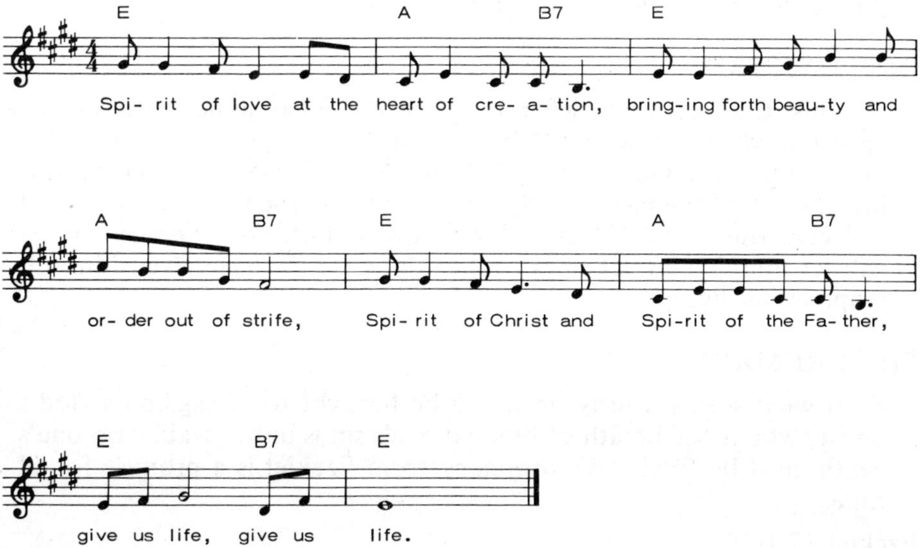

Spirit of love at the heart of creation,
Bringing forth beauty and order out of strife,
Spirit of Christ and Spirit of the Father,
Give us life, give us life.

Spirit of love, the desert now is fruitful,
Dry bones wake to life, and the virgin womb conceives;
Cloud of God's presence overshadows Mary
Who believes, who believes.

Spirit of love who filled the heart of Jesus,
Driving him on to give himself in death,
Spirit of life, give life to us his Body,
By your breath, by your breath.

Spirit of God, cry in us 'Abba, Father!'
Restore in us the image of the Son,
That through your love we find him in each other,
Make us one, make us one.

GREETING

The Holy Spirit is the Spirit of love, of life, of truth: may he be with you to guide your hearts and minds.

INTRODUCTION

At this time of year, we remember the great experience of the apostles, when the Holy Spirit came on them in power, driving them out to bring the Good News of Jesus to the whole world. This is not just a thing of the past: the Spirit, given to us when we were baptised and confirmed, will fill us too with love and life and courage – if we will let him. Today let us try to see how far we have given him full scope in our lives.

FIRST READING

Even what seems utterly dead can be brought to life again by God's Spirit, who is the breath of life. No one's sin is unforgivable; no one's death need be final. This prophecy from Ezekiel is a promise for all time.

Ezekiel 37.1-14

Pause for reflection

SECOND READING

To appreciate that everything is gift, is to begin to understand that the Spirit calls for a different response from everyone. The variety of gifts is a sign of the richness of the giver.

1 Corinthians 12.4-11

Pause for reflection

Song: 'Come, O Spirit' (vv.1,3,4,5) NHS, no.74

GOSPEL READING

The Spirit is given to us so that we may grow in truth and love.

John 14.15-20, 23-27

HOMILY OUTLINE

* Many people today are anxious and bewildered. We need to learn to surrender ourselves in trust to the Holy Spirit, who brings life to the dead and hope to the hopeless.

* We all have different gifts, to be used not for ourselves but for the building up of the Church. What gifts have we been given?

* The Holy Spirit spoke through the prophets, thundering against oppression and injustice. Have we, as laymen, a true concern for social justice?

* The Holy Spirit has been given to us as members of a parish. Is our parish the kind of community that shows Christ to the world outside it?

* The Holy Spirit is the Spirit of truth: what should be our concern, in our own personal lives and as members of the Church, for truth, sincerity and integrity?

PRAYER

The Holy Spirit has been poured out on all of us, to transform us into the likeness of Christ. Let us pray that we may have the courage to be open to him. Let us ask that he may show us the areas in our lives where we fall short.

Pause for silent prayer

God our Father,
you know that we find it easier to be only half-alive,
to stay in the dark, to be content with less than the truth.
Help us to be willing to take the risk
of being open to your Spirit,
to follow where he leads,
knowing that the journey ends in your love
and in perfect union with your Son Jesus Christ.

℟. Amen.

EXAMINATION OF CONSCIENCE

We were given the Spirit when we were baptised and confirmed: we were welcomed into God's family, and given a share in the work of the Church. The Spirit is given to the Church, not to be owned by the Church but so that the Church may bring the Good News to the whole world.

Do we think that this is a job only for bishops, priests and perhaps nuns? Do we say 'but *I* could not preach'?

Do we feel that we have done our part when we have gone to Mass and said our prayers? Do we feel that we are 'supporting the Church' when we help at the parish fete or go to bingo, as if this were the real work of the parish? What should we come to see as the work of the parish?

The Spirit has been given to us to transform our whole lives, so that we may be Christ in the world: what effect has this had on our attitude to our work, our family, our neighbours? to politics? to the Third World?

ACT OF REPENTANCE

If we have been content with the minimum, content just to keep the rules: Holy Spirit, bring us to life.

℟. Holy Spirit, bring us to life.

If we have been inward-looking, concerned only with our immediate family, friends, organisation, parish: Holy Spirit, set us on fire with love.

℟. Holy Spirit, set us on fire with love.

If we have passed over injustice in the Church or in the world, have taken the easy way of unthinking 'loyalty', have been afraid to speak out: Holy Spirit, give us zeal for truth.

℟. Holy Spirit, give us zeal for truth.

If we have turned away so as not to see the needs of others, for fear that we should have to do something about them: Holy Spirit, cure our blindness.

℟. Holy Spirit, cure our blindness.

FINAL PRAYER

God our Father,
we have tried to open our minds and hearts to your Spirit,
so that his light and power
might heal our sins and failings.
Help us to live in the joy of Whitsun,
knowing that your strength
finds its full scope in our weakness.

We make our prayer through our Lord Jesus Christ, your Son,
who lives and reigns with you
in the unity of the Holy Spirit,
one God for ever and ever.

℟. Amen.

BLESSING

May God our Father,
who first breathed his Spirit into man
to make him a living being,
make you fully alive.

℟. Amen.

May Jesus Christ,
who gave the Holy Spirit to his friends
as his first gift after his resurrection,
help you to follow him faithfully.

℟. Amen.

May the Holy Spirit of love
bring you always closer to God
and to each other.

℟. Amen.

And may the blessing of almighty God,
the Father, the Son and the Holy Spirit,
come down on you and remain with you always.

℟. Amen.

CONCLUDING SONG

'Give me joy in my heart' FH Vol. 1, no.78

Confirmed by the Spirit

(for parish groups, in preparation for Pentecost)

ENTRANCE SONG

'Come down O love divine' PTL no.7

GREETING

The grace of our Lord Jesus Christ, the love of God and the fellowship of the Holy Spirit be with you all.

INTRODUCTION

We have just sung together 'Come down, O love divine', and we know that the Spirit who is 'love divine' will certainly come to us. What we are not so certain about is how we will receive him. We know ourselves of old. We know how often we have put obstacles in the way of the Spirit. We know in how many ways we have failed to love. We know that we are sinners. We are here now to express together as a parish our sorrow for past sin. We want to remove every barrier that stands between us and God.

PRAYER

Lord, we come together into your presence this Whitsuntide to prepare ourselves by sincere repentance and prayer to receive anew the gift of the Holy Spirit.

Pause for silent prayer

O God,
give us the experience of the Holy Spirit
working within us.
Grant that we may be enlightened,
purified and strengthened
by your Spirit,
so that we may do your will now and always.
We make our prayer through Jesus Christ our Lord.

℟. Amen.

FIRST READING

The Jews portrayed man's struggle for goodness as a struggle between darkness and light or between the flesh and the spirit, or between death and life. The sinner is the one who prefers walking in the shadows; he is unspiritual and is destined for death. The son of God is the one who lets the light in; he is open to the Spirit and is destined for life. The passage from darkness to light is always a struggle, but it is a hopeful one because the Spirit of him who raised Jesus from the dead is living in us.

Romans 8.9-13

Pause for reflection

SECOND READING

Here St John, in the book of Revelation, gives a picture of those who have persevered through thick and thin, and have won a crown of glory. We should remember that we share Christ's inheritance – provided we are ready to share his life, which is the life of the Spirit.

Revelation 20.4-6

Pause for reflection

Song: 'Bless the Lord, my soul' PTL no.37

GOSPEL READING

It is the Spirit who makes all things new. Those who listen to the promptings of the Spirit will be rewarded a hundred times over.

Matthew 19.27-30

HOMILY OUTLINE

* The struggle in each of us between darkness and light.
* The gift of the Spirit enables us to cope with this struggle.
* Repentance is the beginning of a new life, in other words it is a conversion.
* Repentance gives greater scope for the Holy Spirit to work in and through us.
* The Spirit makes us free of our mistakes and failures, so that we can grow without too many backward glances.

EXAMINATION OF CONSCIENCE

Have we given scope to the Spirit in our lives, at prayer at work and during our leisure?

Have we accepted our responsibilities for the spread of the gospel by praying and working for it? Or have we been afraid we might be asked to do too much?

Do we keep before our minds and the minds of others, hope in the final achievement of God's kingdom, by our Christian love, joy and perseverance?

Do we accept the need for total change in our lives if God's kingdom is to come? Do we recognise such change as the gift of the Spirit?

Do we accept the need to grow continually, and therefore to change continually, even if such growth involves suffering? Or have we been afraid to die to ourselves?

Have we been content to say 'the spirit is willing but the flesh is weak,' without really trying to become more spiritual?

ACT OF REPENTANCE

Jesus said, 'unless I go, the Advocate will not come to you.' Let us pray to the Father through Jesus Christ in the Spirit, the Advocate:

Through Christ in the Spirit you send healing for the contrite.

℟. Lord, be merciful to me a sinner.

Through Christ in the Spirit, you call sinners not the just. ℟.

Through Christ in the Spirit, you forgive our many sins. ℟.

Through Christ in the Spirit, you do not shun the company of outcasts and sinners. ℟.

Through Christ in the Spirit, you carry back to the sheepfold all who have strayed. ℟.

Through Christ in the Spirit, you do not condemn us but send us away in peace. ℟.

Through Christ in the Spirit, you call us to repentance and new life. ℟.

Through Christ in the Spirit, you promise paradise to the repentant. ℟.

PRAYER

May the power of the Father govern us.
May the wisdom of the Son enlighten us.
May the operation of the Holy Spirit quicken us.
O God, we beseech you,
guard our souls, sustain our bodies;
exalt our senses; direct our course;
regulate our manners; bless our undertakings;
fulfil our petitions; inspire us with holy thoughts;
pardon what is past; rectify what is present;
order what is to come;
and all for the sake of Jesus Christ our Lord and Saviour,
who alone can make us perfect as he is perfect.

℟. Amen.

(A prayer of Lancelot Andrewes *Epilogues and Prayers,* Barclay)

BLESSING

May the Lord guide you and make you Christlike.
May the Lord give you his Spirit to recreate you
and give you the power to renew the face of the earth.
And may almighty God bless you,
the Father, the Son and the Holy Spirit.

℟. Amen.

Through Christ in the Spirit
the Lord forgives us and frees us from sin.
Let us go in peace, to love and serve the world.

℟. Thanks be to God.

CONCLUDING SONG

'Come Holy Ghost, Creator come' PTL no.8

Preparation for Freedom

(for parish groups, during Advent)

ENTRANCE SONG

'On Jordan's bank' PTL no.133

GREETING

The Lord will never forget us, and will always care for us tenderly. Let us come to him with faith and love.

INTRODUCTION

The word 'waiting' has a slightly ominous sound – perhaps there is an unconscious association with the dentist's waiting room. Maybe a better word is 'expectation', which has an air of hopefulness about it. Advent is a time when we are expectant – hopefully preparing for the birth of Jesus among us. Part of our getting ready for this birth is making sure we know what sort of household Jesus must be born into, and reassuring ourselves that we, too, have a place in this household. So let us prepare ourselves by praying, by listening, and by reflecting on the way we live.

PRAYER

God the Father loved the world so much that he sent his Son to be our Saviour. Let us pray to God that we may know ourselves and recognise his new-born Son.

Pause for silent prayer

Father,
your love for us is without limit,
and whatever we do or fail to do, you do not forget us.
Help us to break away from the chains of sin,
so that we may discover the freedom of living
as your sons and daughters.
We make our prayer through your Son,
who freely obeyed your will,
Jesus Christ our Lord.

℟. Amen.

FIRST READING

Now let us listen, because God's word is near, if we have ears to hear.

You wait for us
until we are open to you.
We wait for your word
to make us receptive.

Attune us to your voice,
to your silence,
speak and bring your Son to us –
Jesus, the word of your peace.
Your word is near,
O Lord our God,
your grace is near.

Come to us, then,
with mildness and power.
Do not let us be deaf to you,
but make us receptive and open
to Jesus Christ your Son,
who will come to look for us and save us
today and every day
for ever and ever.

You, God, arouse faith in our hearts,
whoever we are.
You know and accept all your people,
whatever their thoughts are of you.
Speak to the world, then, your word,
come with your heaven among us,
give to good and to bad men your sun,
for ever and ever.

(from *Your Word is Near,* Huub Oosterhuis)

Pause for reflection

℟. I will look for the Lord;
God my saviour will hear me.

SECOND READING

The Lord is coming to our homes to heal the broken-hearted, to free those captive to sin or weakness, and to bring joy. To prepare ourselves for this coming we must rake out the weeds and make room for new plants.

Isaiah 61.1-2,10-11

Pause for reflection

Song: 'Make me a channel of your peace' FH Vol.1, no.35

GOSPEL READING

The sign that the Lord has come to our homes is that the blind see, the lame walk, the sick are made well, and the dispirited become joyful. John the Baptist tells us to prepare for this by sorrow for our sins, and turning over a new leaf. He uses a strong image: 'You must lay the axe to the root of the tree.' If need be there must be a radical conversion. Our Lord in praising John says that if we welcome Jesus into our homes we are blessed even more than John was.

Matthew 11.2-11

HOMILY OUTLINE

* God speaks to all – to good and bad alike – and he loves and cares for all. No one need ever give up hope.

* His words invite a reply from us; this reply is our response of faith.

* He gave his Spirit to his Son, who was anointed to serve the world and to bring freedom, joy and hope to those who are in any way enslaved.

* Like Christ we have God's Spirit within us and are anointed to serve each other. Through this service we, too, heal the sick, help the blind to see, and so on.

* Our sinfulness lies in rejecting God's Spirit in favour of our own selfishness. We leave the blind (sick, lame, . . .) as they are because we have not the time, or the energy, or because it's not our business; and we lead astray those who can see, because we have made ourselves rather than God the centre of our lives.

* Forgiveness comes as we root out our selfishness and make room for God. As we prepare to celebrate the birth of Christ in Bethlehem, we should also prepare for his birth in our hearts by seeking forgiveness.

EXAMINATION OF CONSCIENCE

What is there room for in my life? Do I waste my time? Do I clutter up my life with useless activities? Do I waste money on satisfying a craving for things? What is my attitude to money, to material possessions, to food and drink, to clothing? Is my attitude based on what I need, or on what I want? Is my attitude influenced by the material needs of others? Is my attitude the same as Christ's? Am I honest and just in the use of money and property? Do I 'stretch a point' if other people do so also? Do I use my own gifts and talents for myself or for other people? Do I respect my own self, as someone made in God's image and likeness? Do I find it hard to forgive, and to ask for and accept forgiveness? Do I believe that God will never reject me?

Is there room in my life for other people? Do I respect and value other people? How do I treat the members of my family? Do I accept that when I say 'I love you', I take on certain real and practical responsibilities? Do I fulfil these responsibilities? Am I unfaithful to those I love by neglecting them, ignoring them, ill-treating them, or in any other ways? Do I love my neighbour? Do I bother to get to know my neighbour? Ought I to do so? Am I prejudiced about my neighbour because of his colour, class, creed, position, or for any other reason? Do I make other people happy? Do I help people to see better, or to understand more clearly, or to cope more easily with their suffering? Am I my brother's keeper?

Is there room in my life for God? Am I too busy to pay God much attention? Do I keep myself deliberately busy because I am afraid of meeting God too closely? Am I prepared to be silent and to listen when I pray? Do I use words as a smoke screen to keep God at bay? Do I let my doubts frighten me? Do I contribute to the worship of the parish by working for the parish community? Am I satisfied just to be present? Does my passive presence fulfil my obligation to worship? Is religion just a sort of insurance policy for me? Do I worship God with sincerity? Do I worship God throughout the week? Does my daily living give praise to my Creator and Father? Do I live like Jesus Christ, giving myself without limit to my fellow men? Do I do the work of God's Spirit in my daily life?

ACT OF REPENTANCE

Let us now confess our sinfulness together:

I confess to almighty God . . .

May almighty God have mercy on us,
forgive us our sins,
and bring us to everlasting life.

℟. Amen.

Let us pray.

Father,
we pray that through this celebration
we may have grown to a greater freedom
from our selfishness and weaknesses,
so that we are now better prepared
to welcome your Son into our hearts and homes.
We make our prayer through your Son, Jesus Christ, our Lord.

℟. Amen.

CONCLUDING SONG

'O little town of Bethlehem' PTL no.142

BLESSING

May the Lord be born in you today,
and may almighty God bless you,
the Father, and the Son, and the Holy Spirit.

℟. Amen.

The Kingdom of God is at Hand

(for parish groups, during Advent)

ENTRANCE SONG

'O little town of Bethlehem' PTL no.142

GREETING

May Christ cast out our sin, remove our fear, and be born in us today.

INTRODUCTION

Now it is the time for you to wake from sleep, for our salvation is nearer to us than it was when we first believed. The night is ending; the day draws near. Let us then cast off the deeds of darkness and put on the armour of light. Let us live honestly as people do in the daylight, not in carousing and drunkenness, not in lust and debauchery, not in quarrelling and jealousy. But rather let us put on the Lord Jesus Christ and give no thought to the desires of the flesh.

(*Romans* 13.11-12)

PRAYER

Brothers and sisters, we look forward to celebrating the mystery of Christ's coming on the feast of Christmas. Let us pray that when he comes he may find us awake and ready to receive him.

Pause for silent prayer

Lord our God,
maker of the heavens,
as we look forward to the coming of our redeemer
grant us the forgiveness of our sins.

We ask this through Christ our Lord.

℟. Amen.

FIRST READING

God is always inviting us to come to his home. 'Return to me, and I will return to you.' If he sometimes seems a long way off it may be that we are looking altogether in the wrong direction and are deliberately avoiding his searching gaze.

Malachi 3.1-7a

Pause for reflection

SECOND READING

We are waiting for 'a new heaven and a new earth;' we want to be at peace with each other and with the earth. Christ's birth in us, if we, like Mary, accept God's invitation, will effectively bring this peace; but we are free to accept or not, as we will.

Revelation 21.1-8

Pause for reflection

Song: 'Come, Lord Jesus, come' FH Vol.1, no.44

GOSPEL READING

All mankind shall indeed see the salvation of God, but first we must fill in the pits in our own character, smooth off the rough edges, and straighten out the crooked bits.

Luke 3.3-17

EXAMINATION OF CONSCIENCE

A sample examination of conscience prepared by the Congregation for Divine Worship is given on page 163. Other examinations will be found throughout the book.

ACT OF REPENTANCE

Let us confess our sinfulness together.

I confess to almighty God . . .

Now let us say the prayer that Jesus taught his friends.

Our Father . . .

Lord our God,
on the first day of creation
you made the light
that scatters all darkness.
Let Christ, the light of lights,
hidden from all eternity,
shine at last on your people

and free us from the darkness of sin.
Fill our lives with good works
as we go out to meet your Son,
so that we may give him a fitting welcome.

We ask this through Christ our Lord.

℟. Amen.

BLESSING AND THANKSGIVING

May the Father's care protect and guide us.
May his Son be born in us.
May his Spirit of love inspire us.
And may almighty God bless us,
the Father, the Son, and the Holy Spirit.

℟. Amen.

Go in peace,
and proclaim to the world
the wonderful works of God
who has brought you salvation.

℟. Thanks be to God.

CONCLUDING SONG

'Praise to the Lord, the almighty' PTL no.14

The New Standard

(for parish groups, for general use)

ENTRANCE SONG

'Oh Lord my God' FH Vol.2, no.27

GREETING

Brothers and sisters, we have come together in the name of Jesus who made himself our humble servant so that we might find new life. May the new life of our Lord Jesus Christ be with you all and stay with you for ever.

INTRODUCTION

Because his love was without limit Jesus found the strength to give up all pretence to earthly glory. In the end he refused even the admiration and homage of his friends. The one who could have been clothed in gold, receiving tribute from the princes of the earth, chose humility and a cruel death. We are here today so that we can learn a little how to love like Jesus our Lord.

FIRST READING

There is no place for cunning when listening to the word of the Lord. There can be no private places, no reservations, no clever confidence that we will be able to listen and not feel uncomfortable. The word of the Lord is death to our old lives and it must be listened to in simplicity of heart.

Wisdom 1.1-5

Pause for reflection

PRAYER

God our Father,
your Son was born a defenceless child
into this world.
We pray that you will weaken our defences
and open our hearts
so that we might learn to change our lives.

We make our prayer through Christ our Lord.

℟. Amen.

Pause for silent prayer

May the Father of all that is good protect us from distraction so that we may listen in peace and hope.

SECOND READING

It is not enough to be humble in theory, or good only when no action is demanded of us. The followers of Jesus are called to be perfect in action. We are to listen to the words of Jesus and to do what he commands.

1 John 2.3-6

Pause for reflection

Song: 'Thou wilt keep him in perfect peace' FH Vol. 2, no.22

GOSPEL READING

The rule of life for the follower of Jesus is given by Matthew in the Sermon on the Mount. As we listen to each section we can ask ourselves: 'Is Christ saying this to me?'

Matthew 5.21-48

This is a long section of the gospel for just one voice. It would help the congregation if there were several readers, and if there were short pauses after each section of the gospel text.

EXAMINATION OF CONSCIENCE

Let us now examine ourselves in the light of the gospel, humbly calling to mind our sins.

Let us think first of all of the times we have been angry. Have we called other people fools? Have we hardened our anger and refused to forgive? Have we acted according to selfish prejudice? Have we come to the altar of the Lord whilst still retaining anger against our fellow men?

Silent pause

Let us think of the times we have been impure. Have we been ruled by selfish pleasure? Have we treated other people as objects for our own gratification?

Silent pause

Let us think about the times we have been untrue. Have we made promises that we have not kept? Have we failed to speak out so as to correct untruth? Have we hidden the truth for reasons of personal safety or advancement?

Silent pause

Let us think about the times we have sought revenge. Have we tried to get our own back instead of forgiving? Have we spoken ill of those who speak ill of us? Have we failed to love our enemies?

Silent pause

Let us think about the times we have put limits to our loving, and so have failed to strive for perfection.

ACT OF REPENTANCE

Heavenly Father, we have called to mind our sins and now we ask forgiveness from those we have offended. Forgive us for the sake of Jesus Christ your Son. We pray that his living may be the pattern for our future lives.

For the anger and prejudice we have shown to others: Father forgive us and show us your mercy.

℟. Father forgive us and show us your mercy.

For all impurity and selfishness: Father forgive us and show us your mercy. ℟.

For all our untruth and secretiveness: Father forgive us and show us your mercy. ℟.

For the times we have been vengeful and lacking in love: Father forgive us and show us your mercy. ℟.

For the particular faults that we confess to you now in our hearts. *(Pause)* Father forgive us and show us your mercy. ℟.

For the sake of Jesus Christ your Son: Father forgive us and show us your mercy. ℟.

CONCLUDING SONG

'Now the green blade riseth' FH Vol.2, no.14

THANKSGIVING AND BLESSING

With humble hearts we thank you Father
for the gift of your forgiveness;
may the strength that we have gained stay with us
as we strive for perfection in our daily lives.

May the perfection of Jesus Christ
and the spirit of his love go with you,
in the name of the Father,
and of the Son, and of the Holy Spirit.

℟. Amen.

The Peace of Christ

(for parish groups, for general use)

ENTRANCE SONG

'Peace, perfect peace' FH Vol.1, no.2

GREETING

May that peace of God, which is greater than we can understand, guard our hearts and our thoughts in Christ Jesus.

INTRODUCTION

We feel at peace with God and with each other when there is nothing between us to separate us, when we can really speak our minds, knowing that what we say is going to be heard and understood in the way we intend. Many things can prevent this peace of mind. If we have ignored someone or been ignored. If we have hurt someone or been hurt in some way. And so on. We know when we have been hurt by someone else; but we do not always realise the pain we cause others. There is an opportunity for us now to think about how we can discover peace for ourselves and so help to bring peace to others.

PRAYER

Heavenly Father,
guide our minds so that we may see ourselves as you see us.
We pray for the strength to face up to ourselves with honesty,
aware of your presence among us,
through Christ our Lord.

℟. Amen.

Let us now turn to God and pray in the silence of our hearts for the courage to see ourselves as we really are.

Pause for silent prayer

FIRST READING

St Paul tells the Corinthians that they must be cleansed from anyone or anything that makes them unclean, if they want to be the sons and daughters of God.

2 Corinthians 6.14 - 7.1

Pause for reflection

GOSPEL READING

Jesus calls Peter to help him in his work, despite Peter's recognition of his own sinfulness.

Luke 5.1-11

HOMILY OUTLINE

* Peter knew more about fishing than Jesus, but he was able to accept what Jesus suggested even though it did not seem to make sense. This acceptance was the prelude to his recognition of his own sinfulness.

* Jesus's answer was: 'Do not be afraid.' The beginning of peace is self-acceptance and loss of fear.

* Peace finally comes to us when we realise that God is among us; when we trust in him; and when we learn to recognise his actions and his words in the events of our lives.

EXAMINATION OF CONSCIENCE

Have we given ourselves the time to consider what God wants of us?

Have we ignored the ways of finding out what he wants?

De we ever read and reflect on the gospel?

Do we pray regularly?

Do we thank God for what we have been given?

Do we give ourselves the time to listen, to hear what he wants us to do?

Do we choose our friends with care?

Are we popular because we accept too easily things which we know to be wrong?

Do we laugh just because everyone else is laughing?

Are we afraid to follow our consciences?

ACT OF REPENTANCE

℟. Lord forgive us.

When we pretend that we do not need God: ℟.

When our prayer is selfish: ℟.

When we encourage our depression: ℟.

When we are inconsiderate of the needs of others: ℟.

When we fail to help where we see that help is needed: ℟.

When we do not avoid the occasions of sin: ℟.

When we cause temptation to others: ℟.

Let us ask God for his mercy.

'Lord, have mercy' FH Vol.2, one of no.82-85,91

May almighty God have mercy on us, forgive us our sins, and bring us to everlasting life.

℟. Amen.

FINAL PRAYER

Lord here are my hands,
Help me to see them as you see them.
When I am angry, give me your calm.
When I am sad, give me your joy.
When I am afraid, give me your peace.
When I am greedy, help me to be generous,
and to offer myself to you.

℟. Amen.

CONCLUDING SONG

'Hear, O Lord, the sound of my call' FH Vol.1, no.60

Faithful to the Brotherhood

(for the parish council, for general use)

ENTRANCE SONG

'Lead us, heavenly Father, lead us' PTL, no.112

GREETING

Grace and peace to you from God our Father and from the Lord Jesus Christ. The Lord be with you.

INTRODUCTION AND PRAYER

As a group of parishioners there are many things we do together, many things we discuss together. There is the temptation to think that we are doing well because the books are balanced, because the church is cleaned, Mass starts on time, and so on. Today we are going to look at the other side of the parish we represent. How good are we as a Christian community? Do we show our belief that Christ is among us by what we do, by the way we live, by the example we give? We get used to the greeting, 'The Lord be with you.' Let us start by recognising that Jesus is among us now. Let us pray silently for the strength to be honest in our self-examination today and brave enough to follow the road along which Jesus leads us.

Pause for silent prayer

Heavenly Father,
help us to recognise your presence among us,
guiding us and teaching us.
We make this prayer through Christ our Lord.

℟. Amen.

FIRST READING

This reading is a picture of the early Christian community. As we listen to it let us compare it to the picture we present to those who look at us and our parish.

Acts 2.42-47 *(Jerusalem Bible)*

The text could be read as it stands, and then read again sentence by sentence. On the second reading those taking part could be encouraged to make practical proposals for parish life – the proposals merely to be noted, any discussion of them to be left till later.

* 'They remained faithful to the teaching of the apostles.' Do we deepen our understanding of the teaching of the Church? Do we learn to hear and understand so that we may become teachers and witnesses? Do we do enough for those who have no formal education in the faith?

* 'The many miracles and signs worked through the apostles made a deep impression on everyone.'
Do we see ourselves as sources of signs and miracles, impressing the people of this area by our concern for the handicapped, the lonely, the mentally and physically sick, the rejected? Do we seek to perform miracles of healing by our concern, our understanding, our patience? Do we realise that we are being called to do even greater things than Jesus did (see John 4.12)?

* 'The faithful shared among themselves according to what each one needed.'
Are we sufficiently aware of the poor among us, both those close to hand, and those in the Third World? Do we develop skills to support those who are too proud to accept our help? Do we work for justice and peace?

* 'They met in their houses for the breaking of bread. They praised God and were looked up to by everyone.'
Do we invite the lapsed and the weak into our houses for Mass together? Are we afraid to admit that prayer has to be a source of strength in our lives? As a parish do we foster house Masses and prayer groups?

* 'The Lord added to their community those destined to be saved.'
Do we show any responsibility to the non-Christians of our area? Do we seek to understand them and their beliefs or lack of beliefs?

GOSPEL READING

Let us realise that we are here to examine the service that we give to the parish and to the people of this area, as we listen to the gospel reading together.

Luke 17.7-10

ACT OF REPENTANCE

℟. Lord, we are merely servants.

When we discuss the work of our parish, and the needs of this area, may we remember: ℟.

When we meet the lonely, the handicapped or the sick, may we remember: ℟.

When we consider how we care for the poor and the needy here in our parish and throughout the world, may we remember: ℟.

When organising events for our young people, may we remember: ℟.

When sharing in ecumenical worship and inter-church activities, may we remember: ℟.

Let us now say together:

I confess to almighty God . . .

Let us pray.

Pause for silent prayer

Heavenly Father,
help us renew our sense of responsibility
to those we serve in our parish
and in the area in which we live.
By serving each other,
we are serving you, Lord.
Help us to recognise you
when we meet you in others.
We make this prayer, through the servant of all,
Jesus Christ our Lord.

℟. Amen.

Let us go confidently to do Christ's work in our parish.

℟. Thanks be to God.

CONCLUDING SONG

'O God of earth and altar' PTL no.105

Sin and Conversion

(for parish groups, for general use)

ENTRANCE SONG

'To Christ, the prince of peace' PTL no. 182

GREETING

May Christ, who knows our weakness, call us out of our sinfulness; and may his forgiveness be with you all.

673.

INTRODUCTION

St John says that the man who boasts that he is without sin is a liar. If we look at ourselves honestly we soon discover that we have all sorts of attitudes and habits that we are not proud of. This can be a very depressing discovery, because we may have been trying very hard to overcome our weaknesses, and apparently it has all been to no avail. Why keep on trying if it doesn't seem to get me anywhere? The difficulty is that growth to holiness is slow, and in any case cannot be measured. Growth comes when we stop relying on ourselves and begin to rely on God. This is what Peter discovered, as we shall remind ourselves as we listen to three short gospel readings. After each reading we can ask how like Peter's situation our own is.

READINGS AND EXAMINATION OF CONSCIENCE

Peter was sure of himself; whatever anyone else might do he was not going to fail his Lord and Master.

Luke 22.31-34

Do I rely on my own strength, rather than on God who lives in me? Am I too proud to accept help from others? Do I sin because I refuse to see that I am weak? Do I get angry with myself when I sin? Do I say that I am a Christian, but fail to act like a Christian? In what particular ways do I deny Christ?

Pause for reflection

Although Peter had failed to prevent Christ's arrest, he followed from a safe distance. Earlier he had said: 'I would be ready to go to prison with you, and to death.' There was still a chance for him even now to keep his promise.

Luke 22.54-62

Do I follow Christ from a distance, content to do the minimum? Am I afraid to take risks in my following of Christ? Do I compromise or water-down my beliefs so as to make myself more acceptable to others? Am I prepared to let my Christian accent and actions give me away to others, or do I hide my Christianity? When I have sinned am I ashamed to acknowledge my sinfulness? Do I ask for forgiveness from others and from God? Do I forgive others when they deny me? Do I ever let down my friends? In what ways do I express my sorrow?

Pause for reflection

Peter's tears were the sign of his sorrow. Even though he was as weak as any of us, his love of Jesus was genuine and deep; it was simply that he was too reliant on his own strength. The time would come when his actions would match his love.

John 21.15-19

How do I show my love for God? Do I acknowledge my need of him, especially in prayer? Do I feed the hungry, give drink to the thirsty, visit the sick and so on? Do I share my own gifts with other people, so that they can see God's love in me? Am I prepared to be obedient to God's will? Am I really prepared to follow Christ in all things?

Pause for reflection

Let us pray.

Lord Jesus,
you turned and looked on Peter
when he denied you for the third time.
He wept for his sin
and turned again to you in sincere repentance.
Look now on us and touch our hearts,
so that we also may turn back to you
and be always faithful in serving you,
for you live and reign for ever and ever.

℟. Amen.

ACT OF REPENTANCE

God gives us an example of love: when we were sinners he first loved us and took pity on us. Let us turn to him with a sincere heart, and in the words of Peter say to him:

℟. Lord, you know all things; you know that I love you.

Lord, like Peter we have relied on our own strength rather than on your grace. Look on us, Lord, and have mercy. ℟.

Our pride and foolishness have led us into temptation. Look on us, Lord, and have mercy. ℟.

We have been vain and self-important. Look on us, Lord, and have mercy. ℟.

We have at times been pleased rather than saddened by the misfortunes of others. Look on us, Lord, and have mercy. ℟.

We have shown indifference for those in need instead of helping them. Look on us, Lord, and have mercy. ℟.

We have been afraid to stand up for justice and truth. Look on us, Lord, and have mercy. ℟.

We have repeatedly broken the promises of our baptism, and failed to be your disciples. Look on us, Lord, and have mercy. ℟.

Let us now pray to the Father in the words Christ gave us and ask forgiveness for our sins.

Our Father . . .

FINAL PRAYER

Lord Jesus, our Saviour,
you called Peter to be an apostle;
when he repented of his sin
you restored him to your friendship
and confirmed him as the first of the apostles.
Turn to us with love
and help us to imitate Peter's example.
Give us strength to turn from our sins
and to serve you in the future
with greater love and devotion,
for you live and reign for ever and ever.

℟. Amen.

CONCLUDING SONG

'Love is his word' PTL no.75

The Son Returns to the Father

(for parish groups, for general use)

ENTRANCE SONG

'O God of earth and altar' PTL no.105

GREETING

Let us be confident in approaching the throne of grace, that we shall have mercy from him and find grace when we are in need of help. *(Hebrews 4.16)*

INTRODUCTION

It is the willingness and readiness to approach God which is all-important. Our coming here is a sign that we want to grow closer to God. In a moment we are going to hear again the story of the son who left his father, and after reaching the depths of despair said to himself, 'I've been a fool'. It may be that we have never really left God's home, and have never plunged into the real depths of despair, but we have all at some time or another had to say to ourselves, 'I've been a fool'. Such a realisation is the first step to forgiveness; it is the first sign that we are ready to approach the throne of grace.

PRAYER

Let us pray now that we will find God's grace today, and be renewed in faith, hope and love.

Pause for silent prayer.

Almighty God,
you are the Father of us all.
You created the human family
to dwell for ever with you
and to praise your glory.
Open our ears to hear your voice
so that we may return to you
with sincere repentance for our sins.
Teach us to see in you our loving Father,
full of compassion for all who call to you for help.

We know that you punish us only to set us free from evil
and that you are ready to forgive us our sins.
Restore your gift of salvation
which alone brings true happiness,
so that we may all return to our Father's house
and share your table
now and for ever.

℟. Amen.

FIRST READING

God has chosen us to be his adopted sons and daughters. He invites us to live with love as our standard. He wants us to accept forgiveness, so as to become free and able to live gracefully, in Christ Jesus.

Ephesians 1.3-7

Pause for reflection

GOSPEL READING

The son started on his journey home with a prepared speech in his mind: 'Father, I am not worthy to be called your son'. And all the time his father was on the watch for him, and almost before he had time to say his piece was showering him with gifts. This is how God welcomes us. Let us listen to the story peacefully, and let it move us to come to God with confidence, without bothering too much about our set piece; he knows what we want to say, and what is really troubling us.

Luke 15.11-32

HOMILY OUTLINE

* Sin as a turning away from the love that we should have for God our Father.

* The limitless mercy of our Father for his children who have sinned.

* The nature of true conversion.

* The forgiveness we should extend to our brothers.

* The eucharistic banquet as the culmination of our reconciliation with the Church and with God.

EXAMINATION OF CONSCIENCE

This can either be prepared beforehand by the group, or one of the examinations elsewhere in the book may be used.

ACT OF REPENTANCE

Our God is a God of mercy, slow to anger and full of patience. He is the father who welcomes his son when he returns from a distant country. Let us pray to him with trust in his goodness;

℟. We are not worthy to be called your children.

By our misuse of your gifts we have sinned against you. ℟.

By straying from you in mind and heart we have sinned against you. ℟.

By forgetting your love we have sinned against you. ℟.

By indulging ourselves, while neglecting our true good and the good of our neighbour, we have sinned against you. ℟.

By failing to help our neighbour in his need we have sinned against you. ℟.

By being slow to forgive we have sinned against you. ℟.

By failing to remember your repeated forgiveness we have sinned against you. ℟.

Members of the congregation may add other invocations. It may be desirable to have different people saying each invocation.

Let us now call upon our Father in the words that Jesus gave us, and ask him to forgive us our sins, as we forgive each other.

Our Father . . .

FINAL PRAYER

God our Father,
you chose us to be your children,
to be holy in your sight
and happy in your presence.
Receive us as a loving Father
so that we may share the joy and love of your holy Church.

We ask this through Christ our Lord.

℟. Amen.

CONCLUDING SONG

'God is love, his the care' PTL no.276

The Beatitudes

(for parish groups, for general use)

ENTRANCE SONG

'The Lord's my shepherd' PTL no.115

GREETING

May Christ the good shepherd lead us, so that we may come to accept the path of the beatitudes, and so find true happiness.

INTRODUCTION

Christ told us that he had come to fulfil the Law. What he did was to show us that there are no limits to the demands that love makes. Once someone adopts the law of love as his standard he can't ever sit back comfortably and say, 'there's nothing more for me to do'. Today we are being invited to listen to the beatitudes and measure our own lives against them. This will be a motive for encouragement as well as for sorrow.

PRAYER

Let us pray for a moment quietly, asking the guidance of God's Spirit so that we may know ourselves more clearly.

Pause for silent prayer

Lord,
open our ears and our hearts today
to the message of your Son,
so that through the power of his death and resurrection
we may walk in newness of life.

We ask this through Christ our Lord.

℟. Amen.

FIRST READING

All growth is an experience of death and resurrection, and of darkness giving way to light. Some of the time we live in harmony with each other, in the light; at other times there is discord and bitterness, and darkness creeps into our relationships. But if we acknowledge the darkness for what it is – something which estranges us from each other and from God – then God will 'forgive our sins and purify us from everything that is wrong.'

1 John 1.5-9

Pause for reflection

Psalm 145(146).5-10

℟. Happy the man who puts his trust in God.

GOSPEL READING

It is suggested that each beatitude should be read by a different person, together with a brief examination of conscience prepared beforehand, based on the particular beatitude. The reading and examination need to be done slowly and reflectively.

Matthew 5.1-10

ACT OF REPENTANCE

My brothers and sisters, Jesus Christ has left an example for us to follow. Humbly and confidently let us ask him to renew us in spirit so that we may shape our lives according to the teaching of his gospel.

Lord Jesus Christ, you said:
'Happy are the poor in spirit,
theirs is the kingdom of heaven.'
Yet we are preoccupied with money and worldly goods
and even try to increase them at the expense of justice.
Lamb of God, you take away the sin of the world:

℟. Have mercy on us.

Lord Jesus Christ, you said:
'Happy the gentle,
they shall have the earth for their heritage.'
Yet we are ruthless with each other,
and our world is full of discord and violence.
Lamb of God, you take away the sin of the world:

℟. Have mercy on us.

Lord Jesus Christ, you said:
'Happy those who mourn,

they shall be comforted.'
Yet we are impatient under our own burdens
and unconcerned about the burdens of others.
Lamb of God, you take away the sin of the world:

℟. Have mercy on us.

Lord Jesus Christ, you said:
'Happy those who hunger and thirst for what is right,
they shall be satisfied.'
Yet we do not thirst for you, the fountain of all holiness,
and are slow to spread your influence
in our private lives or in society.
Lamb of God, you take away the sin of the world:

℟. Have mercy on us.

Lord Jesus Christ, you said:
'Happy the merciful,
they shall have mercy shown them.
Yet we are slow to forgive
and quick to condemn.
Lamb of God, you take away the sin of the world:

℟. Have mercy on us.

Lord Jesus Christ, you said:
'Happy the pure in heart,
they shall see God.
Yet we are prisoners of our senses and evil desires
and dare not raise our eyes to you.
Lamb of God, you take away the sin of the world:

℟. Have mercy on us.

Lord Jesus Christ, you said:
'Happy the peacemakers,
they shall be called sons of God.'
Yet we fail to make peace in our families,
in our country, and in the world.
Lamb of God, you take away the sin of the world:

℟. Have mercy on us.

Lord Jesus Christ, you said:
'Happy those who are persecuted in the cause of right,
theirs is the kingdom of heaven.'
Yet we prefer to practise injustice
rather than suffer for the sake of right;
we discriminate against our neighbours
and oppress and persecute them.
Lamb of God, you take away the sin of the world:

℟. Have mercy on us.

Now let us turn to God our Father and ask him to free us from evil and prepare us for the coming of his Kingdom:

Our Father . . .

FINAL PRAYER

Lord Jesus Christ,
gentle and humble of heart,
full of compassion and maker of peace,
you lived in poverty
and were persecuted in the cause of justice.
You chose the cross as the path to glory
to show us the way to salvation.
May we receive with joyful hearts
the word of your Gospel
and live by your example
as heirs and citizens of your kingdom,
where you live and reign for ever and ever.

℟. Amen.

CONCLUDING SONG

'Happy the man' FH Vol.1, no.53

God Comes to Look for Us

(for young children, including those who have not yet celebrated the sacrament of penance)

The celebration should be prepared with the children so that they will understand its meaning and purpose, be familiar with the songs, have at least an elementary knowledge of the texts to be read, and know what they are to say and in what order.

GREETING

The celebrant greets the children in a friendly way, reminds them why they have come together and what it is they are going to do.

ENTRANCE SONG

'Come to the Lord' FH Vol.1, no.17

INTRODUCTION

My dear children, we are all God's children. He loves us as a Father, and he asks us to love him. We show we love him if we try to be good and kind to each other. He wants us to live together happily. But people are not always good and kind. Sometimes they hate each other, and turn away from God. This is what we call sin. Even when someone turns away from God, God does not turn away from him. He still loves him, and invites him back again. Listen to what Jesus says about this.

READING

Luke 15.1-7

The people no one else would talk to because they had done wrong, liked to be with Jesus. They listened to what he said. But the 'good' people were angry with Jesus because he made friends with these sinners. So Jesus told them this story: 'Suppose a farmer loses just one of his sheep. Shall I tell you what he does? He leaves the rest of the sheep to look after themselves and goes to look for the one that is lost. And when he finds it he is very happy. He picks it up, carries it home, and tells his friends all about it. Then his friends are happy too. In the same way, when someone is sorry for doing wrong, God and all God's friends are very happy.'

HOMILY

The homily should be short, proclaiming God's love for us and preparing the ground for the examination of conscience.

EXAMINATION OF CONSCIENCE

This should be prepared beforehand with the children, and should be concerned with their immediate lives. It should be a positive examination, looking more to what can be done better, than to what has been done badly.

ACT OF REPENTANCE

God our Father,

Sometimes we have not behaved as your children should.

℟. But you love us and come to us.

We have given trouble to our parents and teachers.

℟. But you love us and come to us.

We have quarrelled and called each other names.

℟. But you love us and come to us.

We have been lazy at home and in school, and have not been helpful to our parents, brothers, sisters, and friends.

℟. But you love us and come to us.

We have thought too much of ourselves and have told lies.

℟. But you love us and come to us.

We have not done good to others when we had the chance.

℟. But you love us and come to us.

Now with Jesus, our brother, we come before our Father in heaven and ask him to forgive our sins:

Our Father . . .

Sorrow may be shown by some sign, for example, individual children may come to the altar or another suitable place with a candle, and light it there. Each child says in his own words a prayer of sorrow. The following is an example:

Father,
I am sorry for all my sins:
for what I have done

and for what I have failed to do.
I will sincerely try to do better.
Help me to walk by your light.

In place of the candle, or in addition to it, the children may prepare a written prayer or resolution and place it on the altar or on a table designated for this purpose.

If the number of children is too great for individual acts of sorrow, the celebrant asks the children to say a prayer of sorrow together.

FINAL PRAYER

God our Father always seeks us out
when we walk away from the path of goodness.
He is always ready to forgive
when we have sinned.
May almighty God have mercy on us,
forgive us our sins,
and bring us to everlasting life.

℟. Amen.

CONCLUDING SONG

'Thank you for giving me the morning' FH Vol.1, no.95

To Make a Better World

(for children, during Christian Aid week)

ENTRANCE SONG

'He's got the whole world in his hand' FH Vol.1, no.29

GREETING

May the love of Jesus, who welcomed children, be with you all.

INTRODUCTION

All of you here today are God's children – and you are lucky children. You have parents to look after you and bring you God's love. You have homes to live in, enough to eat and drink, warm clothes to wear and toys to play with. Some of God's children have none of these things. Even in this country, there are children without homes, and who are hungry and cold. In some of the poor countries, many children are very hungry and cold and lonely. Here is a song about a boy like that.

In a land across the sea,
There's a child that could be me.
His life's a hard and scary game –
Alexander is his name.
  Alexander, tho' I cry
  Tears won't do a thing for you.
  Alexander, I will try
  To make a better world for you.

Alexander has a toy,
A little boat he made from sticks;
He has dreams like any boy –
Alexander's only six.
  Alexander, tho' I cry . . .

No one cares if he is fed,
In the world he's all alone,
Has to steal or beg his bread –
Alexander has no home.
  Alexander, tho' I cry . . .

(*Songs for Young Children,* p.30)

FIRST READING

It's not enough to see pictures of children like Alexander on the TV and to feel sorry for them. It isn't even enough to ask God to feed them. Because how does he feed them? Does he drop bags of rice over India, Africa, China? No, he wants the rich members of his family to help the poor ones. Let's listen now to the story of how Jesus's first friends lived.

Acts 2.42-47, 4.32-37, 5.14-16

They lived together like members of one family. When they had supper together, they broke the loaf, shared it as Jesus had done at the last supper on the night before he died, and remembered what Jesus had done for everybody everywhere.

They spent much time in prayer. They lived together and shared everything with one another. They sold their property and possessions and shared the money out so that nobody went without anything he needed. They were one in heart and mind, and none of them thought that his own things were just for his own use – they were for everybody to share.

(*New World,* Alan Dale, p.166)

Song: *Chorus:* Whatsoever you do to the least of my brothers,
that you do unto me.

When I was hungry, you gave me to eat.
When I was thirsty, you gave me to drink.
Now enter into the home of my Father.
Chorus

When I was homeless, you opened your door.
When I was shivering, you gave me your coat.
Now enter into the home of my Father.
Chorus

When I was laughed at, you stood by my side.
When I was lonely, you gave me your love.
Now enter into the home of my Father.
Chorus

(adapted from FH, Vol.1, no.71)

GOSPEL READING

This is a story about someone who was greedy and wanted everything for himself. He met Jesus, and learned to share.

Luke 19.1-10 (*New World,* p.146)

HOMILY OUTLINE

* Giving and sharing is not easy: it involves sacrifice. By sharing at home and school, we gradually become 'sharing people'.

* Some of us may be greedy, like Zacchaeus. But it is never too late to change. Jesus can help us do this.

* Jesus made friends with Zacchaeus whom nobody liked. God our Father loves us always, even when we are greedy.

* It is good to pray for other people, but our words are empty unless we are prepared to help.

* It's easier to give a penny for a collection for hungry people, than to share our toys, sweets and so on with the people we know.

PRAYER

God our Father has chosen us to be friends of Jesus and live in his way. Let us ask him to help us to see whether we are like Jesus's first friends, or like Zacchaeus before he met Jesus.

Pause for silent prayer

God our Father,
you want us to be like Jesus and his first friends,
kind and generous,
ready to share all that we have.
Let your loving Spirit show us
whether we are sharing people or not,
and make us want to do better.
We make our prayer through Jesus our Friend.

℟. Amen.

EXAMINATION OF CONSCIENCE

Have we been ready to share what we have – toys, books, sweets – with our own brothers and sisters at home?

Have we been ready to share what we have with other children at school? Not just our friends, but the people we don't much like also?

There are other ways of sharing. Have we been generous with our time, ready to help at home or school, even without being asked – even when we wanted to play or watch TV?

When there has been a collection for poor people, have we just asked for money at home, or have we given something from our own pocket-money?

ACT OF REPENTANCE

We have all done wrong: none of us lives all the time as God wants us to. But he loves us always, whatever we do. So we can turn back to him, sure that he has forgiven us.

For the times when we would not share what we had: Father, we are sorry.

℟. Father we are sorry.

For the times when we wouldn't help at home or school: Father, we are sorry. ℟.

For the times when we have been greedy and wanted the best things for ourselves: Father, we are sorry. ℟.

Let us show our willingness to share with each other and to help each other by making a sign of peace.

Sign of peace

FINAL PRAYER

God our Father,
your Son Jesus shared his own loving Spirit with his friends,
so that they might grow more and more like him.
His Spirit is with us too.
May he help us to think more about the needs of others
and less about ourselves,
so that we may give and share as Jesus did.
We ask this for his sake.

℟. Amen.

CONCLUDING SONG

'Spirit of Jesus' (*Sing, Children of the Day,* p.32)

BLESSING

May God our Father,
Jesus his Son,
and their loving Spirit
bless you and help you to grow in love,
today and always.

℟. Amen.

Growing to a New Life

(for children, during Lent)

ENTRANCE SONG

'Christ be beside me' FH Vol.2, no.13

GREETING

May Jesus Christ be with us, now and always.

INTRODUCTION

Jesus said, 'I have come so that you may have more life.' During this time that we are spending together in the presence of Jesus, let us think about this. God gave us life through our parents in the first place, but he also wants us to have more and more life – to grow, to develop our talents, to make the world better, and more beautiful. He calls each one of us personally: 'I have called you by name; you are mine,' he says. Maybe we take no notice, and fail to grow. We shall look at ourselves and see if this is so. And we shall speak to Jesus who is with us and who will show us how to grow.

PRAYER

God our Father,
thank you for the life you have given me.
Thank you for my talents
and for the joy I get out of them.
Help me to use my gifts fully
and through them to make other people happy.

Pause for silent prayer

Lord, you give me everything.
You make me able to think, to act,
to plan, to choose, to love.
You give me life.
I praise and thank you, Lord,
for your gift of life.

℟. Amen.

FIRST READING

Sin is saying 'No' to God's call, or just taking no notice through laziness. St Paul writes about this to the Romans.

Romans 8.8-11

To spell it out simply, there are two ways to live: you can be selfish and do things only for your own pleasure, or you can be a self-giving person, helping others to live good lives. If you live the second way, then you have the Spirit of Jesus in you, and you are a Christian.

(A Children's Lectionary)

Song: 'God delights in his children' FH Vol.2, no.17

SECOND READING

One of the writers in the Old Testament gives us his idea of a great person. We could apply it above all to Jesus, but it shows us, too, what a follower of Jesus (a Christian) should be like.

Isaiah 52.13-53.12

Look at my friend here who serves me. I will make him a great person. Nobody can match my friend in his goodness and helpfulness. He grew up having a great love for God. Actually there is nothing different about his outward appearance. You couldn't pick him out in a crowd, but he has been willing to sacrifice his safety and pleasure to help others. Not many people really appreciate what he has done for them. He is even willing to give up his life if need be to save someone else. That's why I say he is a great person. He loves others more than anyone else I know.

(A Children's Lectionary)

Song: 'Glory to God' FH Vol.2, no.75

GOSPEL READING

Who are the people Jesus calls? In this gospel he tells us.

Matthew 9.9-13

One day Jesus was eating with his friend, Matthew, and some other people who were known to be sinners. Some very righteous people saw them all eating together and enjoying each other's company. While they were watching the dinner party, one of them said, 'How can Jesus be eating with those people? Doesn't he know that they are all sinners? He even seems to be enjoying himself.' Jesus overheard what the man said, so he said loudly enough for everyone to hear, 'People who are healthy don't usually go to see a doctor; sick people do. I have come to call sinners.'

(A Children's Lectionary)

HOMILY OUTLINE

* We are the ones whom Jesus calls; we are all sinners; we often fail.

* Jesus calls us constantly to repent, to change, to grow.

* He says, 'I want to give you more life.'

* Lent is the season of preparation for the great feast of life, of the resurrection of Jesus.

* All around us in nature, too, at this time are reminders of renewed life.

EXAMINATION OF CONSCIENCE

Each of us can ask, 'How do I answer the Lord's call?' Only you can answer that question. It is between God and you.

Spirit of Jesus, give us your light. Help us to see where we fail.

Do we take a few moments every day to be quiet and still, and to speak to God in our hearts?

Do we try to develop our good qualities?

Do we think of others and try to help them?

When we have something difficult to do, do we try hard to succeed?

Do we work with others to do something good and worthwhile?

ACT OF REPENTANCE

For having forgotten you: Lord, we ask your forgiveness.

℟. Lord, we ask your forgiveness.

For not often speaking to you in our hearts: Lord, we ask your forgiveness. ℟.

For not trying: Lord, we ask your forgiveness. ℟.

For using our gifts to hurt others: Lord, we ask your forgiveness. ℟.

For making others unhappy: Lord, we ask your forgiveness. ℟.

God our Father, forgive us.
We have sinned against our brothers and sisters
and against you.
Change us by your Spirit
so that the life and love of Jesus
may grow in us.

℟. Amen.

FINAL PRAYER AND BLESSING

God our Father,
you have made the world and everything in it.
You have made me with my own special gifts and abilities.
I can grow and change; I am alive.
I thank you for this power to grow.
I am sorry for not always answering
your call to grow and to love.
Thank you for your forgiveness.
Lord Jesus you share with me your life.
I thank you and I trust you.

℟. Amen.

May the Lord open our hearts to his call,
so that we may grow in his life and in his love,
now and always.

℟. Amen.

Let us now go in peace, to love and serve the Lord.

℟. Thanks be to God.

CONCLUDING SONG

'In the earth the small seed' FH Vol.2, no.39

Show me the Way

(for young children, during Advent)

ENTRANCE SONG

Advent Song *(Let God's Children Sing,* p.21)

GREETING

May Jesus, the Light of the World, help us to get ready for his birthday.

INTRODUCTION

It's when the evenings and the mornings get darker, and perhaps there are power cuts, that we realise how much we need light. We can't find our way to or from school without street lights, or a torch if we have to go down a country lane. We can't see to read or to play or to find things, unless we switch on the electric light or light a candle or lamp. We can't see what things or people look like; we easily get lost. What do we mean when we call Jesus the Light of the World? (It's easy to use words like that without thinking what they mean.) Jesus came to show us what God our Father is like. Before he came, his own people thought of God as a light guiding them on their journey. This song is about light too, the light of love.

SONG

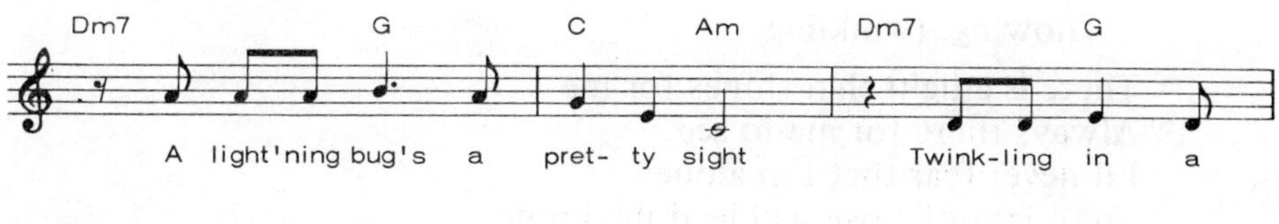

A light'ning bug's a pretty sight
Twinkling in a summer night.
A candle glows and lights a room
A tiny light that chases gloom.
  Glowing, twinkling, burning bright
  in the darkness of the night
  A shining light will lead the way
  And keep me safe till break of day.

A lantern casts a brighter ray
Steady beam to lead the way.
Window shining on the dark
A sight to cheer and warm my heart.
  Glowing, twinkling, . . .

There is a light that shines for me
Always there for me to see.
I'll never fear that I'm alone
The Light of Love will lead me home.
  Glowing, twinkling, burning bright
  In the darkness of the night
  There is a light that shines for you
  To keep you safe your whole life through.

(*Songs for Young Children*, p.48)

FIRST READING

Paul was a person who had lost his way, who didn't really understand what God was like. This is what he said about Jesus:

> God, who made this bright world, has filled my heart with light, the light which shines now I know what he is really like. This was the light which was shining from the face of Jesus.

(see 2 Corinthians 4.6; *New World,* p.218)

Pause for reflection

GOSPEL READING

Jesus is the light who shows us what God is like. Here is the story of how he gave light to someone who had to live in the dark.

Mark 10.46-52; *A Jericho Beggar,* from *New World,* p.35-36

HOMILY OUTLINE

* It is important that we should try to see the meaning of these stories about Jesus. What did this healing mean to the blind man? What does it mean to us?

* We are all blind in different ways: blind to the world we live in, blind to other people. Can we do anything about this?

* Jesus asked the blind man, 'What do you want me to do for you?' He doesn't force us to follow him, to do what he wants us to do. We have to choose.

* Perhaps we would rather stay blind to other people and what they want of us. It's easier and more comfortable, but is it what being friends of Jesus is about?

PRAYER

Let us ask Jesus, the Light of the World, to give us his own loving Spirit, so that we can see what we ought to be doing, and make up our minds to do it.

Pause for silent prayer

Let us sing our prayer together:

Give us light in our hearts, keep us seeing,
Give us light in our hearts, we pray
Give us light in our hearts, keep us seeing,
Keep us seeing till the end of day. (tune from FH Vol.1, no.78)

EXAMINATION OF CONSCIENCE

There are more ways of being blind than having to feel one's way along the roads, like the blind man of Jericho.

We can be blind to all the lovely things in the world, so that we never really look at them:
– but they are all presents from God.

We can be blind to the love and kindness other people show us, so that we never say thank you:
– but they are showing us God's love.

We can be blind to the needs of other people, the people we live with and the people we only hear about; blind to the ways we can help them:
– but Jesus was always ready to help other people, and we are his friends.

ACT OF REPENTANCE

It's easier to be blind sometimes: we don't have to do anything about other people. Jesus can cure our blindness – if we really want him to.

We have passed by the lovely things in God's world, without looking at them properly: Jesus, help us to see.

℟. Jesus, help us to see.

We have not noticed or said thank you for the kindness and help of our fathers and mothers, our friends, our teachers, the people we meet: Jesus, help us to see. ℟.

We have not wanted to see the ways we could help at home or at school: Jesus, help us to see. ℟.

We have not wanted to see the person who was left out, or unhappy, or without friends: Jesus, help us to see. ℟.

THANKSGIVING

Sometimes we have seen all these things: It is Jesus who has given us light to do this. Let us thank him.

For the times when we have seen and enjoyed beautiful things: thank you for your light.

℟. Thank you for your light.

For the times when we have been happy because of other people's love: thank you for your light. ℟.

For the times when we have looked to see what we could do for other people: thank you for your light. ℟.

Christmas is a time when people are kind to us, try to make us happy, give us presents. Let us ask Jesus to help us enjoy his birthday, to thank our families and friends and see how we can make them happy too.

And to show that we are thankful to each other, and sorry for having hurt each other, let us offer one another a sign of peace.

Sign of peace

CONCLUDING SONG

'Give me joy in my heart' verses 1,3 FH Vol.1, no.78

BLESSING

May Jesus fill us with his own light and love
as we get ready for his birthday.
And may God our Father, Jesus his Son,
and their Spirit of Love
be with us and bless us always.

℟. Amen.

Renewal of Our Lives as Christians

(for young people, for general use)

ENTRANCE SONG

'Lord, Jesus Christ, you have come to us' FH Vol.1, no.100

GREETING

May your minds and hearts be renewed, 'so that you can put on the new self that has been created in God's way, in the goodness and holiness of the truth.' (Ephesians 4.23-24)

INTRODUCTION

Friends, we have come here to do penance and to make a fresh start as Christians. Many people see in penance only its difficult side, and its emphasis on sorrow. But it has also a more joyful side, and it looks more to the future than to the past. Through penance God calls us to a new beginning. He helps us to find our true freedom. When Jesus invites us to repentance, he is inviting us to take our place in his Father's kingdom. This is what he teaches us in the parable about the merchant who came across a pearl of great value and sold everything he had in order to buy it. This is not a 'once-only' purchase; new beginnings are a normal part of our growth to maturity. When we find God's kingdom it is too big for us to grasp all at once, and we have continually to adjust our sights so as to enter more fully into it. In doing this we continually die a little to our previous life.

PRAYER

Let us pray quietly for a moment, asking ourselves what we think of as the pearl of great price, for which we would give our all.

Pause for silent prayer

Lord our God,
you call us out of darkness into light,
out of self-deception into truth,
out of death into life.
Send us your Holy Spirit
to open our ears to your call.

Fill our hearts with courage
to be true followers of your Son.
We ask this through Christ our Lord.

℟. Amen.

FIRST READING

At times the struggle in ourselves between good and evil seems almost impossible to bear. We don't understand our own behaviour: we are angry when we would like to be friendly; lazy when in our heart of hearts we want to get the work done; untruthful almost by instinct, even when there is nothing hurtful in the truth. How can we ever improve our behaviour? St Paul writing to the Christians in Rome doesn't give us an answer but only some words of hope. He says that there is bound to be a struggle because there is a tension between the material and spiritual in man. The words of hope he gives are that Jesus Christ is fighting on our side.

Romans 7.14-25

Pause for reflection

GOSPEL READING

The kingdom of God is that community where the qualities of Christ's living – peace and justice, for example – are found. Such a community must be looked for and worked for, it does not just drop into one's lap. When we appreciate the value of such qualities then we are prepared to give our all so as to live them.

Matthew 13.44-46

HOMILY OUTLINE

* The law of sin which in us struggles against God.

* The necessity of giving up the way of sin so that we may enter the kingdom of God.

EXAMINATION OF CONSCIENCE

The details of this should be worked out by the group, but the readings suggest the following reflections.

If I find life a struggle and don't understand myself, do I resolve it by going with the tide? Do I tend to give up the struggle and take the easy way out of things? Am I prepared to work for my growth? Am I arrogant and so pretend to know all the answers? Am I angry with myself when I fail? Am I suspicious of convention to such an extent that I deliberately go against it, just because it is convention? Do I despise those who act conventionally? Do I go all out for obvious material things, and ignore spiritual realities? Do I make time for silence and prayer in my life? What do I regard as really important to me? Do I have a pearl of great price? Am I prepared to work for values that are important to me, or do I only talk about them? . . .

ACT OF REPENTANCE

Christ our Lord came to call sinners into his Father's kingdom. Let us now make an act of sorrow in our hearts and resolve to avoid sin in the future.

I confess to almighty God . . .

Lord our God,
you know all things.
You know that we want to be more generous
in serving you and our neighbour.
Look on us with love and hear our prayer.

Give us the strength to turn away from sin.

℟. Hear our prayer.

Help us to be sorry for our sins and to keep our resolutions. ℟.

Forgive our sins and have pity on our weakness. ℟.

Give us trust in your goodness and make us generous in serving you. ℟.

Help us to be true followers of your Son and living members of his Church. ℟.

God does not want the sinner to die, but to turn to him and live. May he be pleased that we have confessed our sinfulness, and may he show us his great mercy as we pray in obedience to his Son.

Our Father . . .

CONCLUDING SONG

'There is a world' FH Vol.1, no.97

Come, Lord Jesus

(for young people, during Advent)

ENTRANCE SONG

'Come, Lord Jesus, come' FH Vol.1, no.44

GREETING

May the knowledge of Christ's presence be with you all.

INTRODUCTION

In the hymn we have just sung we have prayed that Jesus will come. But he is already with us. His kingdom is within us; where two or three of us are gathered together he is present with us. So often, though, we do not recognise him. The words of the song remind us how great is our need of healing: our hands still do careless work, our eyes do not always shine, and we are dull in heart; our lips do not share the truth, and our feet walk away from others; we live fitfully, half-heartedly and often for ourselves alone. In our prayer we can perhaps see how we can help each other to be enlightened: to see Christ in ourselves and in each other.

PRAYER

Father, we come to you in need of your love. Help us to be open and honest so that we may share our needs.

Pause for silent prayer

Father,
we thank you for offering us your Son
so that our needs may be fulfilled.
Open our ears and hearts to his words
so that we might live more useful and peaceful lives.
We make our prayer through Christ Jesus, our Lord.

℟. Amen.

FIRST READING

When Jesus left his home town he found people living in darkness. He brought them light, and showed them that the kingdom of heaven was already present among them.

Matthew 4.12-17

Responsorial:

This may be read by two readers, or by two groups.

We live in great darkness, Lord:

℟. Lord, give us your light.

We are isolated and alone, Lord:

℟. Come, Lord Jesus, come.

Give us a change of heart, Lord:

℟. And new direction to our lives.

Teach us to be generous and unselfish, Lord:

℟. And to go out to others.

Help us to repent, Lord:

℟. And to recognise your kingdom.

SECOND READING

It is no use saying, 'Come, Lord Jesus,' if we do not recognise his presence in others: to love is to recognise and to respond.

1 John 3.10-20

Responsorial:

Remove our jealousy, Lord:

℟. And let us enjoy the gifts of others.

When we are faced with difficulties, Lord:

℟. Help us not to count the cost.

We pray, Lord, that we may overcome evil with good:

℟. And hatred with love.

Give us gentleness, Lord:

℟. And generosity in speech.

'Make me a channel of your peace' FH Vol.1, no.35

THIRD READING

We are invited to make an honest judgment of ourselves. Do we live as real neighbours of God's friends?

Matthew 25.31-46 and 10.40-42

Responsorial:

The poor man, the outcast, and the sick:

℟. These are my neighbours.

The deprived, the hungry and the naked:

℟. These are my neighbours.

Those who live only for riches:

℟. These are my neighbours.

The depressed, the sad, and the homeless:

℟. These are my neighbours.

My friends and those I love:

℟. These are my neighbours.

These are the people God loves:

℟. These are my neighbours.

ACT OF REPENTANCE

If God loves all these people, he must love me, since I am one of them. We now express our sorrow to God and to each other, because we have not responded to God's gifts. We have been less than what God has called us to be. We have robbed each other and society. In our need, Lord, we pray to you.

When our love for you is insincere and thoughtless: Lord, have mercy.

℟. Lord, have mercy.

When we are afraid of your challenge to our selfishness: Lord, have mercy. ℟.

When we presume on our own strength and do not allow you to speak to us and change us: Lord, have mercy. ℟.

When we prefer darkness to light, close our eyes to you, and choose ignorance: Lord, have mercy. ℟.

When we cut ourselves off from our neighbours who are the lifelines you have sent us: Lord, have mercy. ℟.

When we choose those who please us and so cut ourselves off from most of the population: Lord, have mercy. ℟.

When we look for rewards, using others to boost our self-esteem: Lord, have mercy. ℟.

When we show lack of understanding, walking over the man who is down, dismissing the sad person with a smile: Lord, have mercy. ℟.

When we are impatient, forgetting your patience with us: Lord, have mercy. ℟.

When we judge harshly, and make ourselves unlike you: Lord, have mercy. ℟.

When we are uncritical of society and its superficial values; when we condone evil, and contribute to the suffering of today: Lord, have mercy. ℟.

Lord, we know that you are always forgiving, if we are open to your forgiving love. You heal us through each other. Forgetting and forgiving all the hurts we may have caused each other, and never looking back, let us greet each other with the sign of forgiveness and peace.

Sign of peace

DISMISSAL

Go now, and be alert, and be a neighbour to those in need. Be a light in the darkness; put away shady practices, and let your light shine before men. We have been forgiven much, may we be people of peace and forgiveness.

CONCLUDING SONG

'Colours of day' FH Vol.2, no.1

The Freedom of New Life

(for young people, during Lent)

ENTRANCE SONG

'When Israel was in Egypt's land' FH Vol.1, no.19

GREETING

May the Lord set you free from all sin and selfishness, so that you may find true peace and happiness, now and always.

INTRODUCTION

We have just sung , 'O let us all from bondage flee, and let us all in Christ be free.' During this service of penance we are praying to be freed from the slavery of sin and selfishness. Jesus Christ is our leader on this road to freedom. He leads us to a new life. He leads us where in our heart of hearts we want to be. He leads us to a life of loving and caring for God and for each other.

PRAYER

Let us pray

Pause for silent prayer.

O God,
you call us out of sin and selfishness.
Send the Spirit of Jesus Christ our leader
into our hearts.
In the strength of the same Spirit
may we turn our backs on everything that destroys love.
And may we come to know your freedom and peace.
We make our prayer through Christ our Lord.

℟. Amen

FIRST READING

The story of the Old Testament is the story of how a people came to recognise the helping hand of God. The Jews were often enslaved during their history – by the Egyptians, the Assyrians, the Babylonians, the Romans – and they saw this physical enslavement as a symbol of their enslavement by sin and evil. Likewise their deliverance from slavery they saw as a parable of their march to freedom. The Exodus from Egypt is the great sign of the freedom that comes at God's hands; as it was a sign for the Jews, so it can be a sign for us.

Exodus 14.19-31

Pause for reflection

Song: 'Glory to God' FH Vol.2, no.75

GOSPEL READING

Freedom comes when we are prepared to serve each other. Before his final act of love Jesus washed his disciples' feet saying, 'You must do this to each other.' The service of our neighbour sets us completely free from convention, mere legality, and selfishness.

John 13.2-17

Pause for reflection

Song: 'Oh, the love of my Lord' FH Vol.1, no.79

HOMILY OUTLINE

* The slavery of sin.

* God delivers us from our slavery.

* God delivers us through Jesus Christ.

* God makes us one with Jesus Christ through baptism and repentance.

* Jesus says to us, 'I have given you an example so that you may copy what I have done to you.' (John 13.15)

EXAMINATION OF CONSCIENCE

Do I really face up to my sin and selfishness? Or does my pride blind me to the facts about myself and my condition?

Do I truly believe that God alone can save me? Or do I try to go it alone, thinking that I can lift myself up by my own bootstrings? Do I accept help from others?

Is Jesus Christ really my leader? Do I imitate him? Do I take time off to think about Jesus and pray to him?

Does my baptism mean anything to me? In other words, am I a Christian in the way I think, speak and act?

Do I try to follow Jesus's example and serve those around me? Or am I content always to be on the receiving end?

ACT OF REPENTANCE

If we are slaves to sin, pride and selfishness: Lord, set us free.

℟. Lord, set us free.

If we are tied to the idea that we can save ourselves without you: Lord, set us free. ℟.

If we are easily led, and find little time to think about you and pray to you: Lord, set us free. ℟.

If we are slaves to fashion, and members of a society which does not know you: Lord, set us free. ℟.

If we are servants of self instead of one another: Lord, set us free. ℟.

FINAL PRAYER AND BLESSING

O Lord,
we ask you to give us true freedom
in all our living,
so that we may learn to live more fully,
by living for you and for each other.
We make our prayer through Christ our Lord.

℟. Amen.

The grace and freedom of the Lord Jesus Christ be with you all, now and always.

℟. Amen.

CONCLUDING SONG

'Oh Lord, all the world belongs to you' FH Vol.2, no.66

The Mirror of the Gospel

(for young people, for general use)

This service is intended for small informal groups. The effect will be considerably reduced if the celebrant merely reads out the various sections of the service, particularly the introduction and the examination of conscience. These sections are meant to be guides, not texts.

ENTRANCE

Play softly on a solo instrument or hum to guitar accompaniment the tune 'Plaisir d'Amour' ('My God loves me' FH Vol.2, no.24). The celebrant takes his place in the group. As the music continues quietly he greets those present.

GREETING

My friends, I welcome you here today in the name of Jesus of Nazareth whose love is so great that the very worst of sinners will find comfort in his presence.

A solo singer or a small group sings softly the first verse of 'My God loves me'.

INTRODUCTION

I don't suppose any of you can remember the first time you heard the story about Snow White. Do you remember the wicked queen, Snow White's step-mother? She looked at the mirror and said, 'Mirror, mirror on the wall, who is fairest of them all?' The answer came back, 'Snow White' and we knew then that Snow White was in for a bad time! It was all so simple in those days. The queen was all wicked, and Snow White was all good, and the mirror always told you the truth. We know that the real world is more complicated. When we look in the mirror we see that the battle between good and evil is not just between one person and another, it is within ourselves. We can see some things which are clearly good and some which are clearly bad, but there is also that difficult area in which there seem to be no clear cut answers. A mirror which was really true to life could never give a cut and dried answer like the one given to the queen. It might have said, 'Well, it depends what you mean by "fair". On the surface you've got to admit that Snow White is a good looking girl, but then again she has all the advantages of being a princess. Let's face it, all this stuff about looking after little old men in the forest is a bit too good to be true . . .', and so on. It might be more true to life but it would make a dull fairy story.

Today we are going to try and hold up a truthful mirror to ourselves. We are not going to expect simple answers. We will be looking for what is good and asking for encouragement. We will hope to recognise what is bad and ask for forgiveness. And we will be asking for help in those areas of our lives in which we cannot see clearly what is right, what ought to be done, what is for the best.

PRAYER

First we will spend a few moments in silent prayer. It is enough at this time just to try and relax. We should try to let go of our mental tensions, particularly those which make us concerned about the way we appear to other people.

Pause for prayer, with a background of quiet music.

Father, in heaven,
God of all that is real,
help me to see myself as I am
and not as I pretend to be.
Through Christ our Lord.

℟. Amen.

FIRST READING

Who do you want to be? Do you find yourself being forced into a mould by other people? Here is what Kahlil Gibran wrote in *The Wanderer.*

> It was in the garden of a madhouse that I met a youth with a face pale and lovely and full of wonder. And I sat beside him on the bench, and I said, 'Why are you here?' And he looked at me in astonishment, and he said, 'It is an unseemly question, yet I will answer you. My father would make of me a reproduction of himself; so also would my uncle. My mother would have me the image of her illustrious father. My sister would hold up her seafaring husband as the perfect example for me to follow. My brother thinks I should be like him, a fine athlete. And my

teachers also . . . each would have me but a reflection of his own face in the mirror. Therefore I came to this place. I find it more sane here. At least, I can be myself.'

(from *Readings,* by Denys Thompson, C.U.P.)

GOSPEL READING

It is very difficult to be satisfied with what we are doing. There is always the temptation to look over our shoulder at the next person, thinking that he is much more successful and has all the right answers. There's an illustration of this in an incident involving two sisters, Martha and Mary.

Luke 10.38-42

HOMILY OUTLINE

* The readings illustrate two mirror problems. The first is that other people want us to be a reflection of their hopes and desires. These pressures can be so great that they lead to a rejection of those who are closest to us.

* The second reading illustrates the opposite problem. We wish to appear right and good, and fill ourselves with false expectations so that even the loving act of preparing a meal for guests can become a barrier to a real meeting between ourselves and others.

* We find our truthful mirror in the eyes of those who love us unselfishly. Sometimes it is our parents, sometimes teachers or friends. Through them Jesus can speak to us and if we are willing to relax and listen we will discover all that is good and find forgiveness for all that is evil.

EXAMINATION OF CONSCIENCE

It is time for us to look at ourselves with as much truthfulness as we can muster. It is time for us to be alone with our thoughts. We can pause quietly between each reflection and ask ourselves whether and how it applies to us.

First, we must be willing to seek the truth. We must be ready to open our minds to those aspects of ourselves which we are often afraid to acknowledge.

We might begin by thinking about the people we know who, in their love for us, can show us what we truly are. We might think about the times we have offended them and rejected them because we did not want to admit to the truth.

We can think about the times we have pretended to be what we are not.

There are also times when we are not sure who we are. We don't know how to behave. We don't know what is expected of us. At these times we need to be humble and ready to learn.

There are times when we are caught up in doing something which we know to be wrong. We can't always help ourselves. We need strength, more personal confidence.

There are times when we do things deliberately which we know to be wrong, out of pride, out of anger, out of selfishness.

ACT OF REPENTANCE

Let us ask forgiveness for what we have done wrong, and help to do what we see to be right.

Father in heaven,
through your Son Jesus you showed the world
that no sin is too great to be forgiven.
We open ourselves up to your love
so that what is evil in us will be destroyed
and that what is good in us will grow
into a reflection of your glory.
We make our prayer with him who was raised to glory,
Jesus Christ our Lord.

℟. Amen.

For the times we have pretended when we could have been true: Father forgive us.

℟. Father forgive us.

For the times we have been too proud to listen to criticism: Father, forgive us. ℟.

For the times we have been deliberately proud, or angry, or selfish: Father, forgive us. ℟.

You may wish to add silently a personal prayer for forgiveness for some specific failure:

Pause for reflection. Father, forgive us. ℟.

FINAL PRAYER AND BLESSING

We thank you Father
for the Spirit of love which brings us forgiveness.
May we always live in the light of your truth
and the peace of your forgiveness,
with Jesus Christ our Lord.

℟. Amen.

May the love and peace of Christ
be with you always.
In the name of the Father,
and of the Son,
and of the Holy Spirit.

℟. Amen.

CONCLUDING SONG

'My God loves me', verses 1,2,4 FH Vol.2, no.24

Friendship

(for young people, for general use)

ENTRANCE SONG

'When I needed a neighbour' FH Vol.1, no.41.

GREETING

May the friendship of Christ find a place in our lives, now and always.

INTRODUCTION

We all need friends – they help us to learn about ourselves. This is how God made us. Other people need friends as well, they need our loyalty, our conversation, our help, our companionship. So friendship is not only receiving, it is also giving. Jesus has a lot to teach us about what it is to have friends and what it means to be a friend.

PRAYER

Let us now pray for the strength to see ourselves as we really are. May we be helped to examine how good we are at being friends and how willing we are to change ourselves in order to be friends of God as well as with each other.

Pause for silent prayer.

Father in heaven,
when Jesus was on earth,
he gathered his friends around him and taught them
so that they could help him in his work.
Help us to make good use of our time together today,
so that by deepening our friendship with each other,
we may come closer to you
who live and reign for ever and ever.

℟. Amen.

FIRST READING

St Peter describes how we ought to behave if we want to avoid the condemnation of God.

1 Peter 3.8-12

GOSPEL READING

Jesus explains that our relationship with him depends on whether we do what God wants us to do.

Mark 3.31-35

HOMILY OUTLINE

* Aesop was walking on the road out of Athens. A group of people walking towards the city asked him: 'What are the people of Athens like?' He replied, 'Tell me first, what are the people of your village like?' 'Oh, they are a very unfriendly and impatient lot,' was the reply. Aesop said, 'You'll find that the people of Athens are much the same.' Aesop continued his walk when a second group of people walking towards the city asked him, 'What are the people of Athens like?' He replied, 'Tell me first, what are the people of your village like?' 'Ah, they are very friendly and kind people,' was the reply. Aesop said, 'You'll find that the people of Athens are much the same.'

* Friendship is earned not bought (gospel reading).

* Friendship with God comes through friendship with each other (first reading).

EXAMINATION OF CONSCIENCE

Let us think for a few moments about how good we are at being friends.

Are we honest with them or are we afraid that they might know the truth about us? Do we try to impress them, making out that we are better than we are, or that we are better than they are? Let's think about our honesty towards our friends.

Do we think about our friends when they are not feeling well or when they are sad or upset? Do we remember the things that they like to do, or do we expect them to do what we want? Let's think about how considerate we are towards our friends.

Do we only try to be friends with those who are already popular? Do we show our friendship to the person who is quiet or shy or lonely? Do we defend our friends when they are not around to speak for themselves? Let's think about how choosy and how loyal we are to our friends.

ACT OF REPENTANCE

℟. Lord, help us to be truly sorry.

When we haven't trusted our friends: ℟.

When we haven't told them the truth: ℟.

When we haven't considered their feelings: ℟.

When we haven't been generous or sharing: ℟.

When we've ignored those who aren't immediately attractive: ℟.

When we've been afraid to be loyal: ℟.

Silent pause to express our sorrow.

FINAL PRAYER

Heavenly Father,
your Son Jesus gave up everything for his friends.
He spent his life teaching them and helping them,
and eventually he died for them.
Help us to understand the value
of both giving and receiving friendship,
so that we may become more like your Son,
Jesus Christ our Lord.

℟. Amen.

CONCLUDING SONG

'Follow Christ and love the world' FH Vol.1, no.38

The Truth Will Set You Free

(for students, for general use)

ENTRANCE SONG

'Lord Jesus Christ' FH Vol.1, no.100

GREETING

May the God of Truthfulness enlighten your minds, the grace of Jesus touch your hearts, and the Holy Spirit bring you the gift of self-knowledge.

INTRODUCTION

My friends, we have gathered to think about our sins and about the mercy of God. A sin is not a crime, that is, breaking a law; and it is not a feeling of guilt. A sin is the breaking of our relationship with God and nothing else. So in preparing to turn back to God in an act of repentance, we do not have to go through a rule-book. Nor are we engaged on a therapy which will rid us of guilt feelings. We must see and acknowledge with humility what we have freely done to damage or destroy the bond which holds us close to God as child to Father. We must acknowledge also our faith in God's forgiveness. It is more blessed to give than to receive. But receiving too has its virtue and its difficulty. It requires us to acknowledge our own need and our own inadequacy.

PRAYER

Father,
you have given us the gift of freedom.
Often we have used it wrongly,
acting against your truth and your love.
We wish to turn back to you now,
confessing the past and making a new and deeper dedication
to your service for the future.
Come to us in your silence.
Make us truthful, make us courageous.

Pause for silent prayer.

Father,
your word is near to us,
your love recalls us.
Let the power of your word reach beyond sound
into the deeper places where we are most truly ourselves.

℟. Amen.

FIRST READING

It is sometimes hard to accept that God loves everyone without exception. Jonah thought he was being belittled when God so readily forgave the Ninevites. Here is Jonah's reaction.

Jonah 4.1-11

Pause for reflection

Psalm 50(51)

℟. Against you, you alone have I sinned.

(The Gelineau version of the psalm with the appropriate response may be sung.)

SECOND READING

To say that we have never sinned is to call God a liar, and to show that his word is not in us.

1 John 1.5-10

Pause for reflection

Poem *(read by an individual or a group)*:

Wilt thou forgive that sin where I begun,
Which is my sin, though it were done before?
Wilt thou forgive those sins through which I run,
And do sin still, though still I do deplore?
When thou hast done, thou hast not done,
For I have more.

Wilt thou forgive that sin by which I won
Others to sin, and made my sin their door?
Wilt thou forgive that sin which I did shun
A year or two, but wallowed in a score?
When thou hast done, thou hast not done
For I have more.

I have a sin of fear, that when I've spun
My last thread, I shall perish on the shore;
Swear by thyself that at my death thy Sun
Shall shine as it shines now, and heretofore;
And having done that, thou hast done,
I have no more.

GOSPEL READING

Freedom from sin is a gift from the Father; the gift of truth – the truth will make you free.

John 8.31-38

Pause for reflection

Hymn: *(words for Bach's Passion Chorale)*

Our Father we have wandered
Far from your loving face
In foolishness have squandered
Your legacy of Grace
Now from this half-existence
We rise with fear and shame
And faintly in the distance
We hear you call our name

And now at length discerning
The folly we have done
Behold us Lord, returning
Both prodigal and son
In haste you come to meet us
And home rejoicing bring
In gladness there to greet us
With calf and robe and ring

O Lord of all the living
The lost and the restored
Compassionate, forgiving
And ever caring Lord
Grant now that our transgressing
Our faithlessness may cease
Stretch out your hand in blessing
In pardon and in peace

HOMILY OUTLINE

* The universality of God's mercy. Jonah's refusal to accept this. His response to sin – justice and vengeance. God's answer.

* Yet conviction of God's mercy can be an evasion of moral responsibility: 'If we say we have fellowship while we walk in darkness, we lie . . . we deceive ourselves.' Seeing through our illusions, our wishful thinking.

* 'Fellowship with him', the essence of our lives. Its demands: truthfulness – conviction of sin – humble confession – cleansed from unrighteousness.

* 'The truth will make you free.' Self-knowledge and self-acceptance leading to liberation from inner slavery.

* Self-knowledge not the fruit of morbid introspection. 'He who looks into the perfect law, the law of liberty . . . being a doer who acts.' 'The Son makes you free.' Living in the presence of God's word, translating that word into our lives, the way to freedom and conversion of heart.

EXAMINATION OF CONSCIENCE

General

Sins against God: failure to pray; neglecting public worship; failure to participate intelligently in the liturgy.

Sins against others: positive unkindness; negative failures to care and to help; using others as means for our own satisfaction. Neglect of family.

Sins concerning ourselves: pride, conceit and vanity; not taking proper care of ourselves; staying up too late too often, not eating regularly. Drink, drugs.

Specific

Our student work; superficiality, downright neglect. Failure to respect truth; writing, talking, arguing for victory or for effect. Failing to listen to others. Cultivating scepticism and doubt. Failing to grow to an intelligent, mature faith. Contempt for simple people.

Social and political involvements. Excess or defect? Playing a game in politics. Failure to be just to unfashionable views. Loving mankind rather than your neighbour. Opting out of social problems and student politics. Fear of taking an unfashionable line on topical problems.

Interpersonal matters. Being swept away by permissiveness; lack of personal moral seriousness; sexual irresponsibility in various forms.

Failure to build up the Church in the student community; opting out of its mission there and in the wider world. Failure to work at bridging the gap between the student church and parish life.

ACT OF REPENTANCE

Father, we acknowledge our sins with shame, we look to your mercy with hope.

Father forgive us, although we know very well what we did. Lord, have mercy.

℟. Lord, have mercy.

Father, we wish to come to you with more than our shame; with more than our trust in your forgiveness. Let us come to you with a thorough-going self-surrender to your call. Christ, have mercy.

℟. Christ, have mercy.

Father of infinite mercy, do not look any longer at our past. Our future lies in your hands. Make it a new beginning. Lord, have mercy.

℟. Lord, have mercy.

Lord in your providence, all things cooperate for good; even in a mysterious way, our sins. Let the recognition of these sins be a lesson we learn about ourselves and about your word. Let it be for us another claim on your love. Lord, hear us.

℟. Lord, graciously hear us.

FINAL PRAYER AND BLESSING

Dear Father,
all our hope is in you.
Give us the grace of reconciliation
with you and with each other.
Enlighten our minds, renew our hearts;
give us your strength to heal our weakness,
your power to re-kindle our courage.
We ask this through Jesus Christ our Lord.

℟. Amen.

May the Lord bless you and keep you.
May he make the light of his countenance to shine upon you
and give you peace.

℟. Amen.

CONCLUDING SONG

'Lord of all hopefulness' PTL, no.288.

The Fellowship of Forgiveness

(for students for general use)

ENTRANCE SONG

'Yahweh, you are my strength' FH Vol.2, no.63

GREETING

The grace of our Lord Jesus Christ and the love of God and the fellowship of the Holy Spirit be with you all.

INTRODUCTION

It is one of the best things about the times we live in that the value of the individual is recognised as never before. It is one of the disasters of the time that individual freedom, pursued at the expense of the caring community, leads so often to separation, isolation and death. As followers of the living Christ we are gathered here to be reconciled to each other and to our Father in heaven so that we may find our personal freedom in the love and care of our brothers and sisters in Christ.

PRAYER

Let us pray.

Pause for silent prayer.

Father in heaven,
your love is the gift above all gifts,
the flowering of all that has been created.
Strengthen us with your Spirit.
Let us risk all that we possess,
so that we might be touched by your love
and in that freedom discover our new selves.
In the name of Jesus Christ, your Son and our Lord.

℟. Amen.

MEDITATION AND READINGS

We will now watch and listen to a dramatisation on the theme of separation and reconciliation. This is not a play for our entertainment, but a meditation and an aid to self examination. During the meditation, following the lead of the choir, we all sing quietly, 'Lord, have mercy'. (eg, the Israeli Mass, FH Vol.2, no.85).

A group of young people stand in a circle with a girl at the centre crouching down. They begin to move round slowly and sing quietly 'Poor Jenny lies a weeping'. (Different parts of the country will have different versions of this song.)

Poor Jenny lies a weeping, a weeping, a weeping,
Poor Jenny lies a weeping on a bright summer's day.
Stand up and choose your loved one . . .

At this point they stop moving and singing. The girl in the centre goes to each one in turn to 'choose' them. But one by one they reject her saying such things as . . .

. . . I wouldn't lower myself
. . . We'll do it my way
. . . I just can't be bothered
. . . I can't stand them near me
. . . I want it for myself, I *will* have it
. . . It should be mine

Finally the girl from the centre rejects them all, saying:

'I'm better on my own.'

(These lines are meant to be a guide. Each group can make up its own lines to suit circumstances.)
Each person in the group then makes a further move away from the others indicating by what they say that they are not going to forgive or make a conciliatory move.

. . . Why should it always be me?
. . . I never get my own way
. . . It's just not worth making the effort
. . . I don't care about them anyway
. . . It's not fair
. . . They're just jealous
. . . I don't need any of them

The person saying the lazy line (the third in this example) lies down on the floor as he or she says the line. They remain still in these attitudes of rejection. A group of boys who have been standing by moves forward. One goes round looking at the 'statues' ending with the girl lying on the floor. He looks round and then says:

'Your sins are forgiven you.'

The rest of this group turn away saying such things as:

. . . Who does he think he is?
. . . The man blasphemes
. . . Arrogant nonsense

The boy playing Jesus looks at them and says:

Which is it easier to say,
Your sins are forgiven you,
or, take up your bed and walk?

Silent pause

He looks at the person lying on the floor and says:

Take up your bed and walk.

He slowly stands and walks away. As he does so the choir begins to sing 'Lord, have mercy'. The whole group begins to move round, singing with the choir. They do not meet each other's eyes but they arrange themselves in a group behind Jenny who crouches down in her original position. They remain still during the reading which follows.

Colossians 3.1-15

The last few verses of the reading are spoken chorally. (That is, members of the group say them to each other; they do not all speak at once.)

You should be clothed in sincere compassion
in kindness and humility,
gentleness and patience,
bear with one another;
forgive each other as soon as a quarrel begins.
The Lord has forgiven you,
now you must do the same.
Over all these clothes and to keep them together
and complete them, put on love.
And may the peace of Christ reign in your hearts,
because it was for this that you were called
to be parts of one body.

While they are saying these lines the whole group forms a circle around Jenny again. As they finish she stands and chooses her loved one. She is accepted into the circle which begins to move round as they hum the 'Poor Jenny' tune again. The circle breaks and they lead off to take their seats in the congregation. As they sit down the tune fades into silence. There should be a long silence followed by the gospel reading.

Matthew 25.31-46

HOMILY OUTLINE

* The primacy of love and the demands it makes on our everyday relationships with others.

* The necessity of joining ourselves to others particularly when the institutions and educational processes so often emphasise individual achievement and competition.

* The way in which Jesus is alive to us today in the needs of others, in our own needs, in our love and affection.

* The need to recognise where we have offended and are in need of forgiveness. The offence can paralyse us but to each one Jesus says, 'Take up your bed and walk'.

EXAMINATION OF CONSCIENCE

In the consciousness that we are all in need of forgiveness let us think first of all of those who are closest to us. Think about those who depend on us for affection and a sense of their own value. Have there been times when we have ignored them or sought to diminish them so that we might appear better than we are?

Let us consider now the people we work with, those we may not call our special friends but who are connected with us through common interests and the accident of circumstances. They do not require food and clothing and shelter from us, but they do require recognition in their work, human contact and sympathy in their chosen line of study. As we think of these people let us consider the times we may have offended them by being over-competitive, by depreciating their efforts, by underestimating their potential, or by ridiculing their struggles.

Let us above all consider those times when we have chosen isolation rather than communication, perhaps by burying ourselves in either work or leisure activities and ignoring the needs of those around us. Have there been times when we have been content to be Christians in theory only, concerned with distant objectives and ready to ignore the practical demands of the world?

ACT OF REPENTANCE

Let us pray.

May the Lord God almighty, whose perfection is the judge of all our actions and whose love is the hope of our forgiveness, help us to know how we have offended and to express our sorrow for our sins.

For the times we have rejected those who are close to us: Lord, have mercy.

℟. Lord, have mercy.

For the times we have refused to forgive: Lord, have mercy. ℟.

For the times we have isolated ourselves, and refused practical help where needed: Lord, have mercy. ℟.

For the times we have considered only our own work and leisure, and have refused to see the talents and the difficulties of others: Lord, have mercy. ℟.

If there are specific failures for which we want forgiveness let us bring them to mind now. *(Pause)* Lord, have mercy. ℟.

Let us now pray together for forgiveness in the words Jesus taught his friends:

Our Father . . . (sung version, FH Vol.1, no.89)

BLESSING

May the peace of Christ reign in your hearts,
so that joined in love we may be parts of one body.
In the name of the Father,
and of the Son,
and of the Holy Spirit.

℟. Amen.

CONCLUDING SONG

'Sing my soul' FH Vol.1, no.62

There are dangers in the sort of dramatised meditation described here. The main one is that the event will have about it the aura of a performance. This can be avoided by reducing the acting to its very simplest elements. For example, the words of Jesus should be spoken as straightforward direct statements; they do not require any histrionics or obvious dramatic emphasis. All movement should be simple and quite slow. At the end of a performance we often feel the need to applaud, but at the end of this sort of dramatisation there should be a deep, reflective silence.

A Call to Service

(for students, during Lent)

ENTRANCE SONG

'Said Judas to Mary' FH Vol.1, no.48

GREETING

The grace of our Lord Jesus Christ, and the love of God and the fellowship of the Holy Spirit be with you all.

INTRODUCTION

One of the events mentioned in the gospel story before the passion account begins is the anointing of Christ's feet by Mary Magdalen. This story inspired the writing of the song we have just sung. The words serve to remind us that we are at one with Mary Magdalen. We are at one with her in being called to serve the poor of the world who are the body of Jesus Christ; there is a poor man, a needy man, in every man. It is with a sense of failure in our vocation that we have come together. We are deeply conscious that we have not served the poor. We have not served Jesus Christ. We have come into the presence of the Lord sorry and repentant, determined by his power to change.

PRAYER

Let us pray.

Pause for silent prayer.

O Lord,
we ask you to grant us a true sorrow for our sins.
We ask you to forgive us,
and give us the strength
to follow the Lord Jesus in all things.
We make our prayer through the same Jesus Christ,
your Son and our Lord.

℟. Amen.

FIRST READING

Whatever our guilt we can always have hope. The first movement towards holiness is having a sense of sin. As we begin this lenten service let us join together in one of the greatest of the penitential psalms.

from Psalm 50(51) *(said together by everybody present):*

> Have mercy on me, God, in your kindness.
> In your compassion blot out my offence.
> O wash me more and more from my guilt
> and cleanse me from my sin.
>
> My offences truly I know them;
> my sin is always before me.
> Against you, you alone, have I sinned;
> what is evil in your sight I have done.
>
> O see, in guilt I was born,
> a sinner was I conceived.
> From my sins turn away your face
> and blot out all my guilt.
>
> Give me again the joy of your help;
> with a spirit of fervour sustain me,
> O Lord, open my lips
> and my mouth shall declare your praise.
>
> For in sacrifice you take no delight,
> burnt offering from me you would refuse,
> my sacrifice, a contrite spirit.
> A humbled, contrite heart you will not spurn.

Pause for reflection

'Were you there?' FH Vol.1, no.99

GOSPEL READING

The passion of our Lord Jesus Christ according to John.

John 18,19 *(This can be read by several people, or dramatised.)*

EXAMINATION OF CONSCIENCE

John asks us to recognise the divine in Jesus. He draws our attention to the divine with his remark, 'they moved back and fell to the ground', after Jesus had said, 'I am he'. Do we recognise the divine in Jesus

Christ and make him the centre of our living? Do we recognise the divine possibilities in the poor we meet? Do we make this possibility a reality by encouragement, support, example and the service of the poor? Do we recognise the divine possibility in ourselves and make it a reality by openness to God who speaks to us in all our experience? Do we pray and thereby engage in man's highest activity? *(Pause for reflection.)* Lord, have mercy.

℟. Lord, have mercy.

Jesus said, 'If I am the one you are looking for, let these others go'. Jesus protects his own from destruction as he promised he would. Do we protect our own? Do we protect our family? Do we neglect our family? Do we make a real effort to communicate with older (or younger) members of our family and community? Are we conscious of the impact of our way of life on those younger than ourselves? *(Pause for reflection)* Lord, have mercy.

℟. Lord, have mercy.

Jesus said, 'Put your sword back in its scabbard; am I not to drink the cup that the Father has given me?' Do we reject or shirk the implications of the Christian way of life, that to live we must learn to die? Do we try to avoid the cup that the Father has given us? Do we work an eight hour day? Do we try to build the pattern of death and resurrection into our lives by self-denial? Or must we admit, 'I haven't done a thing about Lent so far this year'? *(Pause for reflection.)* Lord, have mercy.

℟. Lord, have mercy.

'Now Judas the traitor was standing among them.' Do we stand with Christ or are we fair weather Christians? How does our regard for the poor stand up in the face of betrayal by the poor? Do we quickly say, 'That's the last thing I'll do for her'? Are we prepared to love and serve even if we are crucified by ingratitude and thanklessness? Do we ever play the traitor and betray our Christian trust by self-centred ignorance of those around us? *(Pause for reflection.)* Lord, have mercy.

℟. Lord. have mercy.

'Again Peter denied . . . and at once a cock crew.' Are we, like Peter, irritating to our friends with our continual boasting, more or less subtle? Can we only be Christian when we are roused? Does our so-called Christianity take a violent turn, condemning all around us?

Do we stand our Christian ground quietly and fully in the courtyard of our lives, at prayer, at work, and at play? Or are we constantly saying 'I am not one of this man's disciples', by giving up prayer, settling for shoddy work, and not really giving ourselves at leisure time – like the spoiled child always having to be coaxed and cajoled? *(Pause for reflection.)* Lord, have mercy.

℟. Lord, have mercy.

Pilate belonged to the world that rejects the light. Indifference to the truth, indifference to the light, is the equivalent of rejecting the light. Had Pilate been a man of truth he would have freed Jesus. Instead he began a series of compromises that led to Jesus's execution. Are we indifferent to the truth, the truth about ourselves, the truth about living? If we must confess to indifference, constantly putting persons, situations and questions to one side, we must confess too, that we have rejected the truth in some measure. How much reading, thinking and discussion do we involve ourselves in about persons, and things for which we are responsible? We cannot live fully on inane and unrelieved chatter. *(Pause for reflection.)* Lord, have mercy.

℟. Lord, have mercy.

Pilate persists in calling Jesus the King of the Jews, to goad the Jews, unable to pass up these additional opportunities of taunting the people he hates. Do we ever taunt, or goad, or hate? *(Pause for reflection.)* Lord, have mercy.

℟. Lord, have mercy.

'We have no King but Caesar.' Pilate finally goads the chief priests who want Jesus's death no matter what the cost, into repudiating their proudest possession, their religious and national heritage. Do we ever repudiate our religious heritage? Are we ashamed of our background? *(Pause for reflection.)* Lord, have mercy.

℟. Lord, have mercy.

ACT OF REPENTANCE

Pilate yields to the demand that Jesus be crucified. Even in death Jesus remains in command of the events and says, 'Father forgive them; they do not know what they are doing'. So in great confidence and joy we confess to almighty God that we have sinned, and seek his forgiveness.

We confess that we have failed in our Christian vocation, each in our own way.

We confess that we are deeply conscious that we have not served the poor, we have not served the Lord.

We confess that we have failed to love.

We confess that 'anyone who fails to love can never have known God, because God is love'.

We confess that we are in a state of alienation and sin. But we know that this sorrowful admission is the death of self and leads to resurrection and the fulness of life.

Let us kneel and together confess to almighty God and to each other that we have sinned.

I confess to almighty God . . .

Now let us offer each other the sign of peace.

Sign of peace.

FINAL PRAYER AND BLESSING

Grant, O Lord God,
that we may be faithful to you without parting,
worship you without tiring,
serve you without failing,
always seek you,
happily find you and be with you,
the one only God, world without end.

℟. Amen.

(The prayer of St Anselm)

May the grace, mercy and peace of God,
the Father, the Son and the Holy Spirit,
come down on us all,
and remain with each one of us always.

℟. Amen.

CONCLUDING SONG

'Give me joy in my heart' FH Vol.1, no.78

I Am the True Vine

(for religious, during Lent)

ENTRANCE SONG

'Oh the love of my Lord' FH Vol.1, no.79

GREETING

The Lord loves us with an everlasting love: let us trust in the gentleness of his mercy.

INTRODUCTION

At this time of year, we remember especially that Jesus bore our sins, so that we might be forgiven and filled with his Spirit. By that Spirit we are united to the true Vine without whom we can bear no fruit. We have come together to look at our lives in the light of his life and teaching.

FIRST READING

Let us begin by listening to the extraordinary prophecy of Isaiah, about the sufferings of the servant of Yahweh, and ask ourselves what is implied by the question, 'Who could believe what we have heard, and to whom has the power of Yahweh been revealed?'

Isaiah 52.13 - 53.5

Pause for reflection.

Responsorial song:

Keep in mind that Jesus Christ has died for us,
and is risen from the dead.
He is our saving Lord,
he is joy for all ages.

BHP, p.26

SECOND READING

St Paul writes to the Christians at Rome (and to people in all ages) about the inward struggle in us between what he calls the 'spiritual' and the 'unspiritual'. He then reminds us that the struggle is not a hopeless one, because we have been possessed by God's Spirit.

Romans 8.8-18

Pause for reflection.

Responsorial song:

Grant to us, O Lord, a heart renewed;
recreate in us your own Spirit, Lord.

BHP, p.38

GOSPEL READING

If we belong to Christ and are willing to be possessed by the Spirit we must expect to be pruned. This will enable us to bear rich fruit, fruit that will last.

John 15.1-11.

HOMILY OUTLINE

* The meaning of virginity 'for the sake of the kingdom of God'.

* Bearing fruit: prayer and apostolate.

* The vine and the branches: an image of community?

* The role of religious in the whole body of Christ; religious life as a particular living out of the common baptismal vocation and commitment.

PRAYER

Those who follow Jesus are to be united with him in the self-giving love which made him the Man for Others. Let us pray that we may see where we fall short in our following of him.

Pause for silent prayer.

God our Father,
every day we pray that your will may be done,
and your will for us is that we be transformed
into the image of your Son.
In your great respect for our freedom
you wait for our consent.
Send your Holy Spirit into our minds and hearts.
May he give us the light
to see where we have failed in love,
and the love to turn back to you for forgiveness and strength.
Through Jesus Christ our Lord.
℟. Amen.

EXAMINATION OF CONSCIENCE

We have been called to serve God in the religious life, not for our own sakes but that we might work with him for the coming of his kingdom on earth. All the gifts God gives are to be shared with others. He has given us special gifts: have we borne the fruit we should?

Have we failed in single-minded obedience to the word and will of God?

Have we failed in our service of others? Has our love been self-centred?

Have we failed in the bearing of each other's burdens, which should be the distinguishing mark of our community life?

ACT OF REPENTANCE

If we have made our work an idol, an end in itself, forgetting that we are not simply teachers, social workers, . . . Lord, we ask for mercy.

℟. Lord, we ask for mercy.

If we have allowed our household to become, not a community sharing everything, but a collection of individuals following their own way: Lord, we ask for mercy.

℟. Lord, we ask for mercy.

If we have allowed our life as religious to insulate us from the everyday needs and concerns of our neighbours: Lord, we ask for mercy.

℟. Lord, we ask for mercy.

If we have made either our community life or our work the excuse for not being available to serve others when and where they needed us: Lord, we ask for mercy.

℟. Lord, we ask for mercy.

If we have refused to come to terms at a deep level with our tensions and dilemmas, but have sought instead easy and superficial solutions: Lord, we ask for mercy.

℟. Lord, we ask for mercy.

'Yes, I shall arise' BHP, p.20,21.

FINAL PRAYER

Loving Father,
we know that you welcome with joy
all who sincerely turn back to you.
Forgive us our failures
and help us to commit ourselves again
to the following of your Son in self-giving love.
We make this prayer through him,
and by the power of the Holy Spirit.

℟. Amen.

BLESSING

May God our Father transform you from glory to glory, into the perfect likeness of his Son.

℟. Amen.

May Jesus Christ, who forgave his faithless friends, keep you always in his friendship.

℟. Amen.

May the Holy Spirit, the love of the Father and Son, set you on fire to carry that love wherever you go.

℟. Amen.

And may the blessing of almighty God,
the Father, the Son and the Holy Spirit,
come down on you and remain with you always.

℟. Amen.

CONCLUDING SONG

'In him we see the God' *The Heart of a Rose, p.25*

Love is for All Seasons

(for nuns, during Advent)

ENTRANCE SONG

'Where love and loving kindness dwell' PTL, no.188

GREETING

The grace and peace of God our Father and the Lord Jesus Christ be with you.

℟. Blessed be God, the Father of our Lord Jesus Christ.

INTRODUCTION

Winter is waiting and promise. Its word is often unspoken. Sometimes, too, it is sorrowful and finds itself alone.

Winter knows that love is coming – and wants it to come. It feels the pull of longing. It looks up to the sky and out to the hills and the sea. And then it begins to snow.

Love in winter is cold outside and warm inside; ice skating and fireplaces; snow and mittens.

Love in winter is Christmas. God becomes involved with us. His word becomes flesh. He offers peace.

In winter love asks to be open, to be honest and to trust. Listen to love in winter.

(Listen to Love, p.14)

'God becomes involved with us. His word becomes flesh.' God continues to become involved with us and with all men through us and through all men. 'Where love and loving kindness dwell, there God will ever be;' God will ever be becoming more closely involved with us. Sadly, we do not allow God to become involved with us, because we sin and fail to love. All this we acknowledge: our flagrant infidelities, our mediocrity and our lack of surrender to love. All this we repent. We are sorry and seek the forgiveness of the God who is love.

PRAYER

God invites us to conversion. Let us ask him for the gift of true repentance.

Pause for silent prayer.

Heavenly Father,
we seek your forgiveness.
Forgive us for the times we have failed to do
the things we knew to be right.
Forgive us for the times we have failed to love
and so have prevented your coming to us and to all men.
Forgive us for the times we have refused to serve others,
and so have refused to serve you.
Forgive us for our failure to be what you call us to be.
We make our prayer through Christ our Lord.

℟. Amen.

FIRST READING

That God is the God of love, and the God to love, is at the basis of Jewish tradition. This reading from Deuteronomy came to be the most important of all Jewish prayers, the *Shema.* This passage is referred to by Jesus as the greatest commandment of the Law.

Deuteronomy 6.4-9

Pause for reflection.

'The coming of our God' PTL, no.134

SECOND READING

In this well-known passage from his letter to the Corinthians Paul talks to all of us. He talks about love -- that which binds man to man, and man to God.

1 Corinthians 13.1-13

Pause for reflection.

'God is love' PTL, no.276.

GOSPEL READING

To answer the Pharisee's question, 'Which is the greatest commandment of the Law?' Jesus quotes two texts of the Law. These two texts are the foundation of the gospel way of life.

Matthew 22.34-40

HOMILY OUTLINE

* Advent, the time of preparation for the coming of the Lord.

* God, the Creator, has been involved with his work of creation from the beginning of time. The climax to his involvement with us was the Incarnation: the Word was made flesh.

* God continues to come. The Word is continually made flesh in those who live in unselfish love.

* Jealousy, boasting, conceit, selfishness, resentment, dishonesty and so on stop God coming to his own.

* The virtue of penance opens the way for the coming of the Lord.

EXAMINATION OF CONSCIENCE

Let God's living word, a two edged sword, search our hearts:

'Love is always patient and kind.' *(Pause)*

'Love is never jealous.' *(Pause)*

'Love is never boastful or conceited.' *(Pause)*

'Love is never rude or selfish.' *(Pause)*

'Love does not take offence and is not resentful.' *(Pause)*

'Love takes no pleasure in other people's sins, but delights in the truth.' *(Pause)*

'Love is always ready to excuse, to trust, to hope and to endure whatever comes.' *(Pause)*

ACT OF REPENTANCE

God is love. God is infinite mercy. He pardons all who repent. He takes away their guilt. Let us have every confidence in God and ask him to forgive us all our sins.

In your love, Lord, forgive us our sins against community love.

℟. Lord, have mercy.

In your love Lord, forgive us our sins against individual love.

℟. Lord, have mercy.

In your love Lord, forgive us our sins against love in the Church.

℟. Lord, have mercy.

In your love Lord, forgive us our sins against love of the stranger.

℟. Lord, have mercy.

In your love Lord, forgive us our sins against love of the very young.

℟. Lord, have mercy.

In your love Lord, forgive us our sins against love of the very old.

℟. Lord, have mercy.

FINAL PRAYER AND BLESSING

To God the Father,
who first loved us and made us accepted in the Beloved:
To God the Son,
who loved us and washed us from our sins in his own blood:
To God the Holy Spirit,
who sheds the love of God abroad within our hearts:
Be all love and glory,
For time and for eternity.

(The Ascription of Thomas Ken)

And may the blessing of almighty God,
the Father, the Son and the Holy Spirit,
come down on us and remain with us for ever.

℟. Amen.

CONCLUDING SONG

'O come, O come, Emmanuel' PTL, no.131.

She has Chosen the Better Part

(a Marian service of penance for a pastoral community)

ENTRANCE SONG

'Hail, O star that pointest' HYC, no.29.

GREETING

May the Lord Jesus, Son of God, born of Mary by the overshadowing of the Spirit, be with us now and always.

INTRODUCTION

During this time together we shall ponder in our hearts the mystery of that authentic woman of whom Paul speaks in the earliest reference to our Lady in the New Testament. 'When the appointed time came, God sent his Son, born of a woman, born a subject of the law, to redeem the subjects of the law and to enable us to be adopted as sons.' (Galatians 4.4-6). The mystery of Mary is the exemplar of the mystery of each of us, and in a special way of every woman – the mystery of personhood, of the creative and separating love of God, of the bringing forth of Christ in the darkness and the conflict of faith. Mary, the great contemplative, 'pondered in her heart' the mystery in which her simple, ordinary and laborious life was plunged. We are 'busy about many things', as demanded by our apostolic mission to be directly involved in the work of the Church. But our first call is to be contemplative, to look on the world from that 'heaven of the heart' where Jesus espouses us in faith.

PRAYER

Holy Spirit, whose power overshadowed Mary, deepen in us the habit of contemplation, of pondering in our hearts as she did the mystery of Christ.

Pause for silent prayer.

Father,
as Mary opened her being to the Word of God,
we ask that everything should be done to us
according to your will.

We make our prayer in the name of him
who was obedient in all things,
Christ Jesus our Lord.

℟. Amen.

FIRST READING

The Annunciation

Nothing will ease the pain to come
Though now she sits in ecstasy
And lets it have its way with her.
The angel's shadow in the room
Is lightly lifted as if he
Had never terrified her there.

The furniture again returns
To its old simple state. She can
Take comfort from the things she knows
Though in her heart new loving burns,
Something she never gave to man
Or god before, and this god grows

Most like a man. She wonders how
To pray at all, what thanks to give
And whom to give them to. 'Alone
To all men's eyes I now must go,'
She thinks 'And by myself must live
With a strange child that is my own.'

So from her ecstasy she moves
And turns to human things at last
(Announcing angels set aside).
It is a human child she loves
Though a god stirs beneath her breast
And great salvations grip her side.

Elizabeth Jennings

(or extract from Northumbrian Sequence IV, by Kathleen Raine, in *A Christian's Prayer Book,* p.37.)

Responsorial song:

'You are the honour' BHP, page 51.

SECOND READING

From the beginning Mary is identified with the praying Church.

Acts 1.12-14.

Pause for reflection.

Acclamation:

'The Lord has done marvels for me' HYC, no.98.

GOSPEL READING

Mary treasured the revelation of Jesus as it came to her and pondered it in her heart.

Luke 2.15-20.

HOMILY OUTLINE

* Mary, the woman totally responsive to God's initiative (Luke 1.26-38).

* Mary, the woman of courageous affirmation (Luke 1.46-55).

* Mary, the woman of intuitive compassion and practical action (Luke 1.39-45; John 2.1-12).

* Mary, the woman of faithful endurance (John 19.25-27).

* Mary, the Mother (Luke 2.42-62).

* Mary, our advocate.

* 'The modern woman will note that Mary of Nazareth was far from being a timidly submissive woman; on the contrary, she was a woman who did not hesitate to proclaim that God vindicates the humble and oppressed and removes the powerful of this world from their privileged position.' (Paul VI, *Marialis Cultus).*

* Not alone thou hearest when thy name we hail;
Often thou art nearest when our voices fail;
Mirrored in thy fashion all creation's good,
Mercy, might, compassion grace thy womanhood.

(Dante, *Divina Commedia)*

EXAMINATION OF CONSCIENCE

In the light of Mary of the gospel, I ask myself how I use my talents:

Do I embrace things and persons in their wholeness?

Do I respond generously to challenging initiatives?

Do I cultivate an intuitive and practical compassion?

Are my decisions personal and concrete, rather than abstract?

Am I receptive?

Do I pray, as distinct from giving time to prayer?

In short, to what extent am I available?

ACT OF REPENTANCE

For my failure to meet people where they are: Lord, I ask forgiveness.

℟. Lord, I ask forgiveness.

For my self-protectiveness: Lord, I ask forgiveness. ℟.

For my fear of being hurt, deceived, and exploited: Lord, I ask forgiveness. ℟.

For my denial of the generous impulse: Lord, I ask forgiveness. ℟.

For my legalism: Lord, I ask forgiveness. ℟.

Lord, you showed your glory to the world in the child-bearing of Mary. May we respond to your word as she did and be filled with the Holy Spirit.

FINAL PRAYER AND BLESSING

God our Father,
Mary gave birth to a Son
who offers salvation to the whole world.
May we, like her, both treasure him in our hearts
and bring him to all men.

℟. Amen.

May we go forth, rejoicing in the power of the Spirit.
And may almighty God bless us,
the Father, the Son and the Holy Spirit.

℟. Amen.

CONCLUDING SONG

'Maiden yet a mother' HYC, no.46

Poverty, Chastity and Obedience

(for religious, on the anniversary of their consecration)

ENTRANCE SONG

'I love you, Lord, my strength' Psalm 17(18).2-7

GREETING

Seek Yahweh,
all you, the humble of the earth,
who obey his commands.
Seek integrity,
seek humility:
you may perhaps find shelter
on the day of the anger of the Lord. (Zephaniah 2.3)

℟. Lord, who shall we go to?
You have the message of eternal life, and we believe;
we know that you are the Holy One of God. (John 6.68)

The Lord says: 'Come to me, all you who labour and are overburdened and I will give you rest. Shoulder my yoke and learn from me, for I am gentle and humble in heart, and you will find rest for your souls. Yes, my yoke is easy and my burden light.' (Matthew 12.28-30)

INTRODUCTION

We are invited to grow like Jesus, who was the humble and poor servant of Yahweh; his love for his friends was pure and without egoism; he came to do his Father's will and was obedient to death. We remember that these gifts of poverty, chastity and obedience are for the people, gifts to be shared. None of us has lived up to Christ's example, so let us be ready to learn, and respond to Christ's call to our next point of growth.

PRAYER

Father, your Son became poor so that he could be the friend of the least. His love reflected your free and total love. His faithful commitment to your will and his lack of self-interest led him to lay down his life for his friends. Listen to the prayers of your weak and tired servants who wish to serve you better.

Pause for silent prayer.

We have been chosen from the least to be servants of the poor. We now greet the words of our King in the gospel, by asking for the joy of poverty, the peace of purity, and the love of obedience.

'Give me joy in my heart' FH Vol.1, no.78

FIRST READING

The Father prepared a wedding feast. Jesus took the lowest place, and his Father raised him to the place of honour.

Luke 14.7-14

Pause for reflection.

Psalm 17(18).17-24

SECOND READING

We have been consecrated to love excessively: a love that is catholic, universal, and total.

Matthew 12.46-50.

Pause for reflection.

Psalm 17(18).25-31

THIRD READING

Obedience is to drink the cup; to follow God's will, the joy of service without thought of reward; to be careless in loving.

Matthew 20.20-28

Pause for reflection.

Psalm 17(18).32-37

EXAMINATION OF CONSCIENCE

Poverty

Do I consider myself to be above anyone else? Am I patronising in my attitude to others? Do I acknowledge my weaknesses? Do I approach others from below, or ride roughshod over them? Am I courteous in the use of my gifts? Am I open to being helped? Am I willing to learn? Do I invest in belongings and surround myself with distractions? Am I generous with myself and with my goods? Am I willing to arrive late in heaven with my brothers and sisters, or am I over-anxious about my own soul?

Chastity

Do I use my vows of chastity as an excuse not to be involved with people? Have I become a platonist in my relationships? Am I afraid of affection and human warmth? Does my vow enable me to love many, as well as much? Do I play off love of God with love of neighbours? Have I remained human enough to understand another's difficulties? Do I complain when I find the cross is the price of loving much? Am I willing to learn by my mistakes? Do I love only those who love me? Am I patient with wounded people? Is my love free or is there a price others must pay for my friendship? Is my love divisive or exclusive? Do I share my friends or am I possessive? Am I willing to accept love? Have I become selfish: a pampered spinster, or peevish bachelor? Do I realise and am I compassionate with the agonies of married people? Am I married to the community and to God's people?

Obedience

Have I used my vow as an excuse for servility? Have I turned my superior into a god, accrediting him with infallibility? Am I honest with those who care for me? Do I wait to be told what to do or do I take the initiative in following God's will? Have I the charity to confront my superiors if necessary? Do I rob my community by being a conformist? Am I willing to sacrifice my preferences for the common good? Am I faithful to God's call or am I always looking back? Do I resent the gifts that I have been given? Do I act as part of the community or am I committed to no one?

ACT OF REPENTANCE

Father,
we thank you for having chosen us
from the least of your peoples
to be servants like your Son.
We ask forgiveness for our failures to remain poor,
for the selfishness of our love,
and for the inconsistency of our obedience.
Teach us your ways and renew our hearts
so that we may be a greater gift for the world.

℟. Amen.

FINAL PRAYER

Father,
we thank you for this annual reminder of our consecration.
Stir up the grace and generosity
that was within us on that day.
May we grow always in your love,
and become true disciples of your Son.

℟. Amen.

CONCLUDING SONG

'My soul magnifies the Lord' Luke 1.46-55

Lest in Preaching to Others

(for priests, for general use)

ENTRANCE SONG

'Dear Lord and Father of mankind' PTL, no.100

GREETING

May the grace of our Lord Jesus Christ, the loving welcome of the Father and the inner prompting of the Spirit be with you.

INTRODUCTION

Brothers, we who are ministers of this sacrament of forgiveness know ourselves to be unprofitable servants. We know ourselves also to be sinners. Once we were called and chosen. Once we answered that call. Often we have failed to match our lives to our call. Often we have failed to imitate what we enact. In this liturgy we strive to listen to God's call again as it comes to us in the Holy Scriptures. We strive to recognise and to acknowledge our failures. Most importantly, we turn our hearts back to God and rededicate ourselves to our calling.

PRAYER

Father, we have sinned against heaven and before you. We are not worthy to be called your sons. Listen to us attentively Lord, as now we ask you for the grace of repentance.

Pause for silent prayer

Father,
your word is near us,
your love recalls us.
Give us the grace to listen to you,
not with our ears only but with the whole of our hearts.

℟. Amen.

FIRST READING

A parable is for all time. We may not have committed David's sin, but we can all hear Nathan's simple words – not an accusation but a statement: 'You are the man.'

2 Samuel 12.1-7a ('. . . you are the man.')

Pause for reflection.

Psalm 129(130)

℟. In you Lord, is my hope.

Hear this appeal, Master of my life
Out of the darkness where my spirit dwells
Hopeless, unless you turn your gaze
Attentively towards me. ℟.

If it is my sins that catch your eye
Truly, my case is desperate;
But yours is a forgiving love
Therefore, though fearfully, I come to you. ℟.

In you Lord is my hope
At your word my spirit quickens. ℟.

As the weary watchman on the ramparts
Strains his eyes for daybreak,
More eagerly than he my sleepless heart
Awaits your coming. ℟.

Because your name is mercy
And all your ways compassionate.
Because the sins of your people
Dissolve in your healing love. ℟.

SECOND READING

It is easy to become buried in our work and yet not be buried with Christ. Our resurrection comes as we learn to die to sin.

Romans 6.1-14

Pause for reflection

Canticle:

℟. Alleluia.

Salvation and power and glory belong to our God
His judgments are true and just ℟.

Praise our God all you his servants
You who fear him small and great ℟.

The Lord our God the almighty reigns
Let us exult and rejoice and give him glory ℟.

The marriage of the Lamb has come
And his bride has made herself ready ℟.

GOSPEL READING

At times of repentance we are glad to have come to our senses again. As we listen to this story about God's mercy we can ask ourselves what we really set our hearts on, and if this is a falling short, whether we are prepared to say to God, 'Father, I have sinned against heaven and against you.'

Luke 15.11-24

Pause for reflection

Hymn: 'Our Father we have wandered' (see page 106).

HOMILY OUTLINE

* Responsibility: how readily we attribute it to others – 'You are the man.'

* The law: a fact and a necessity, but not the source of morality – our relationship with God is that.

* The law: never a source of salvation – God's grace through our faith is that.

* Wasting our substance in a far country: talents and qualities lying idle – not used in the service of God and our neighbour.

* 'I will return': two movements: away from sin and towards the Father.

* 'At a distance, his Father saw him': never beyond the horizon of God's mercy.

* 'He ran to meet him': grace the first initiative – ours to respond.

EXAMINATION OF CONSCIENCE

The basic question

'He who is not for me is against me.' What is our basic direction?

We must not stop at externals. Sin is from the heart. Our fundamental response to our vocation – is it weakening, is it failing to grow?

Sins against God

Are we allowing idols to take his place – a person? persons? work? ease? enjoyment? things? money?

Failure to worship: our own participation in liturgy? our work in liturgy for others? our attitude to liturgy? failure in private prayer?

Our vocation as his ministers: laziness? failure to keep abreast with things? self-seeking in our ministry?

Failure to hope? relying on ourselves? not trusting?

Sins against our neighbour

Those we live with: intolerance? lack of understanding? failure to support them? failure to visit the sick or unhappy?

Those we are responsible for: hoarding our time? impersonality? excessive firmness, excessive flexibility or inconsistency?

Sins against chastity which harm others: emotional entanglements? using people for our own satisfaction?

Failures in our mission: involvement with the local community? social responsibility?

Sins against ourselves

Pride, vanity, or conceit?

Sins against chastity which harm ourselves and damage our single-mindedness?

Sins against poverty: unnecessary luxury? selfish bachelorhood?

Failure to study? Intellectual pride or escape into study, or into drink or hobbies or television?

Self-pity? Indulgence or daydreams? Failure to keep in touch with reality?

ACT OF REPENTANCE

Lord, against you, you alone have we sinned, we ask your pardon: Lord, have mercy.

℟. Lord, have mercy.

We have closed our ears to your call, our eyes to your light, we ask your pardon: Christ, have mercy.

℟. Christ, have mercy.

We have let selfishness grow and govern our lives. We ask your pardon: Lord, have mercy.

℟. Lord, have mercy.

We have turned our back on you, we have failed in our calling. We rise, we turn again, we ask you to come to meet us: Lord, hear us.

℟. Lord, graciously hear us.

FINAL PRAYER

Master,
you have brought us back within the arc of your grace.
Through the mystery of your Son's death and resurrection
in which we so closely share,
keep us now and always in the safety of your love.
We ask this through Jesus Christ our Lord.

℟. Amen.

May the Lord bless you and keep you.
May he make the light of his countenance shine on you
and give you his peace.

℟. Amen.

CONCLUDING SONG

'Now thank we all our God' PTL, no.93.

The Servant of All

(for priests, on retreat)

ENTRANCE SONG

'O God our Father' PTL, no.297

INTRODUCTION

Jesus is the eternal priest and everlasting king, the fulfilment of all prophecy. We have been consecrated to share for ever in his work. We have not reached the end. We come together to thank God for what he has done through us, and to support and encourage each other as we continue our journey together. We listen to his word which comforts and confronts us so that we may grow in holiness, in wisdom and in service. Jesus is our anchor, the sure source of our hope. At the start of our prayer of sorrow let us listen to the author of Hebrews.

Hebrews 6.9-20

Pause for reflection

PRAYER

Jesus,
you have asked us to use our gifts
generously in your service.
You have invited us to share your priesthood
as a gift, for the service of others.
Make us holy, so that others may be holy.
Give us a gentle, courteous and courageous tongue
so that others may hear the Good News.
Help us to share your kingship by humble service.
Give us your Spirit so that we may learn to follow your ways.
We now pray to you quietly for forgiveness.

Pause for silent prayer

Father,
be merciful to us,
who are poor instruments of your peace.
Enlighten our minds, increase our faith,

give us the joy of knowing that we work for you,
and especially give us a share of your love for men.
We make our prayer through your Son, Jesus Christ our Lord.

℟. Amen.

FIRST READING

We have been anointed because we, like all men, are still searching and are still in need. We are weak, ignorant and lacking in faith. By our wounds many may be healed, if we will pray without ceasing.

Hebrews 5.1-10

ACT OF REPENTANCE

For considering myself superior to others: Lord, have mercy.

℟. Lord, have mercy.

For not allowing or encouraging the laity to play their full part in the parish: Lord, have mercy. ℟.

For my impatience with the ignorant: Lord, have mercy. ℟.

For refusing to be the friend of sinners: Lord, have mercy. ℟.

For turning prayer into a duty, or neglecting it altogether: Lord, have mercy. ℟.

For being a talker and not a listener in prayer: Lord, have mercy. ℟.

For talking about suffering, but being unwilling to suffer: Lord, have mercy. ℟.

For saying 'This is my body given for you', but failing to give myself to others: Lord, have mercy. ℟.

For not preparing myself for the celebration of the sacraments: Lord, have mercy. ℟.

For careless and insensitive celebrations of Mass: Lord, have mercy. ℟.

For being more interested in numbers of converts, communicants, and penitents, than in the quality of my attention: Lord, have mercy. ℟.

For complaining about the lack of vocations, without acknowledging that my own life, and lack of joy and faith may attract no one to the priesthood: Lord, have mercy. ℟.

For my laziness, lethargy and indulgences: Lord, have mercy. ℟.

For my lack of faith, hope and love: Lord, have mercy. ℟.

For allowing myself to be taken in by pagan and worldly values: Lord, have mercy. ℟.

For guarding my popularity and being unwilling to be abused and criticised: Lord, have mercy. ℟.

For being a 'sanctuary priest' whose liturgy is a lie: Lord, have mercy. ℟.

For my littleness and parochialism: Lord, have mercy. ℟.

For choosing canon law instead of the gospel: Lord, have mercy. ℟.

For living by rubrics and not by the Holy Spirit: Lord, have mercy. ℟.

For my lack of personal discipline: Lord, have mercy. ℟.

SECOND READING

Shepherds must provide good food and clear water. Prophets must share God's love for people, and must be in contact with God's word so that the good news they preach will be to the point and life-giving. Priests must be great teachers, otherwise they can expect this confrontation with the Lord.

Ezekiel 34.1-16

ACT OF REPENTANCE

We have failed to study the scriptures: Christ, have mercy.

℟. Christ, have mercy.

Our preaching has been dull, unprepared and lifeless: Christ, have mercy. ℟.

We have scolded the people for their ignorance even when it has been caused by our own sins of negligence: Christ, have mercy. ℟.

We have been interested in practising Catholics, with no mind for the countless others: Christ, have mercy. ℟.

We have taught people without first learning: Christ, have mercy. ℟.

We have counselled many without seeking counsel for ourselves: Christ, have mercy. ℟.

We have been selective in the places we have visited; we have not eaten with sinners, nor gone to the places that sinners frequent: Christ, have mercy. ℟.

We have sat in presbyteries and expected people to come to us: Christ, have mercy. ℟.

We have spoken in formulas and cliches because we have not bothered to know the truth: Christ, have mercy. ℟.

We have not used modern means of communication to further the spread of the gospel: Christ, have mercy. ℟.

We have been afraid of being considered unorthodox, and have failed to proclaim the light that is within us: Christ, have mercy. ℟.

We have run away from the lot of the prophet: Christ, have mercy. ℟.

THIRD READING

As sharers in the bishops' rule of the Church, we are not to rule as the pagans do. The greatest must be the least. We are not to lord it over others. Our rule is to serve. Our yokes must be gentle and our burdens light. Do we practise the aggressive power of the Pharisee or the humble service of Christ?

Matthew 23.13-36 and John 13.1-16

(these two passages may be read by several readers)

ACT OF REPENTANCE

If we forget that with the bishops we are the least in the kingdom: Lord, have mercy.

℟. Lord, have mercy.

If we hamper the work of the Spirit in other people, and have harried or bullied God's people: Lord, have mercy. ℟.

If we take care of the sanctuary, but neglect the living sanctuary that is another person: Lord, have mercy. ℟.

If our rule in the parish is autocratic and self-opinionated: Lord, have mercy. ℟.

If we have failed to learn from the laity and other priests: Lord, have mercy. ℟.

If we have neglected other Christian communities and members of other world religions: Lord, have mercy. ℟.

If we have sat in judgment on the faith of our fellow priests: Lord, have mercy. ℟.

If by our lack of love we have hastened another's departure from the priesthood: Lord, have mercy. ℟.

If our treatment of curates, students for the priesthood, and nuns has made them feel of little worth: Lord, have mercy. ℟.

If our presbyteries are not Christian homes, but hostels for strangers: Lord, have mercy. ℟.

If we fail to love our fellow priests: Lord, have mercy. ℟.

If we fail to love those entrusted to us: Lord, have mercy. ℟.

If we have failed to be humble: Lord, have mercy. ℟.

If we have misused our power: Lord, have mercy. ℟.

If we have obeyed the letter of the law without regard to the spirit of the gospel: Lord, have mercy. ℟.

If we have condemned or judged another: Lord, have mercy. ℟.

If we have failed to be honest or to cooperate with each other, especially with our bishop: Lord, have mercy. ℟.

If we have been hypocritical: Lord, have mercy. ℟.

If we presume to be greater than our Master: Lord, have mercy. ℟.

If we fail to walk with the poorest – anywhere, at any time: Lord, have mercy. ℟.

PRAYER

Lord Jesus,
we are ashamed of our record of failure;
we acknowledge our sins with sorrow and ask for forgiveness.
Help us to rely on your strength and your Spirit.
As you forgive us, help us become
true ministers of your forgiveness to others.

Let us now turn to the Father who always forgives, and pray to him in the words the first priests learned:

Our Father . . .

BLESSING

Blessed are you, Lord God of all creation;
through your goodness we have been chosen to serve mankind.
May we become, through Jesus Christ, a source of life and love.

℟. Blessed be God for ever.

And may almighty God bless us,
the Father, the Son and the Holy Spirit.

℟. Amen.

CONCLUDING SONG

'When I needed a neighbour' PTL, no.298

Hope is Founded on Patience

(for school chaplains and teachers, during Advent)

ENTRANCE SONG

'O come, O come Emmanuel' HYC, no.52

GREETING

May we rejoice in the coming of Christ, now and always.

INTRODUCTION

Hopeful and alert waiting is a biblical theme, and is that of the Church during the season of Advent.

> We wait for birth. We wait for love. We wait for life to reveal its meaning, year by year, experience by experience. Waiting is the law of life, the measure of love. To wait for another person is to be willing to be alone for him. To wait together with another is to form a community of hope with him.
>
> An understanding of Jesus begins with a theology of patient expectation. Jesus must be awaited. He comes to patient hearts, to those willing to be alone as they wait. Jesus is the other awaited by those who form a community of hope and become watchful for signs of his approach.
>
> Projects may be rushed, schedules can be accelerated, but life will not be hurried. No life happens without waiting. This does not mean that one must be quiescent or that life comes to the inactive. It means that time-tables serve the momentary and relatively unimportant events of life. Life, however, does not occur on schedule.
>
> *Dawn without Darkness,* Anthony T. Padovardo

Hopeful, creative, vigilant waiting makes up a great part of the religious educator's role, and it is often difficult. To encourage, but not force, growth, to await signs of readiness for a new stage, asks more of us than does organising, administering, dogmatising.

PRAYER

God our Father,
show us how, as religious educators,
to wait on your action
both in ourselves and in our children.
Teach us how to form with them a community of hope,
through Christ our Lord.

℟. Amen.

Pause for silent prayer

Lord Jesus,
you are the awaited one.
You are also the one who waits.
Together we seek to answer your call.

℟. Amen.

FIRST READING

Jesus is awaited by history, by men who have faith in him. Men's faith has faltered; they have been faithless. But God is faithful. The sign of his faithfulness, the sign that he will be with us, is a child.

Isaiah 7.10-14, or *I am coming soon* by Eric Milner-White *(A Christian's Prayer Book, p.34)*

Pause for reflection

Response: 'Maranatha' BHP, page 7.

SECOND READING

We now hear a lyrical reciprocation of the cry 'Come!'

I am coming soon,
and bringing my recompense with me,
to requite everyone according to his deeds.

I am the Alpha and the Omega,
the first and the last,
the beginning and the end.
I am the scion and offspring of David,
the bright star of dawn.

'Come!' say the Spirit and the Bride,
'Come!' let each hearer reply.
Come forward, you who are thirsty;

accept the water of life,
a free gift to all who desire it.

He who gives this testimony speaks;
'Yes, I am coming soon!'
Amen. Come, Lord Jesus!

Revelation 22.12-13,16-17,20

Pause for reflection

Acclamation:

Amen.
Alleluia, alleluia.
Come, Lord Jesus, come.
Alleluia.

GOSPEL READING

We listen to the account of Mary's waiting, and how Jesus came to be born.

Matthew 1.18-25

HOMILY OUTLINE

* Jesus also waits – to be born of Mary, to grow, to learn to talk. to meet the Spirit.

* Waiting is essential to the life of the Spirit.

* The bridegroom opens the door to those prepared to wait.

* The father who waits finds his prodigal son.

* The gospel urges us to wait and says that the watchful are blessed.

* In school, we try to build up a community of faith, hope, and love, a situation in which Jesus will be enabled to 'come' repeatedly through the experience of shared activity, shared liturgy, shared prayer.

* Children need time to realise themselves, to grow in relationship with others, with God.

EXAMINATION OF CONSCIENCE

Are the pupils the centre and starting-point of plans, lessons, and school liturgies?

Am I willing to await, to encourage, and to serve the signs of their growth?

Am I trying to develop in the school a community of hope?

Am I patient, free from fear, and ready to change?

ACT OF REPENTANCE

When our hope and courage flag: Lord, have mercy.

℟. Lord, have mercy.

When we fail to listen: Lord, have mercy. ℟.

When we lose patience: Lord, have mercy. ℟.

When we fall back on formulas: Lord, have mercy. ℟.

When we do not love: Lord, have mercy. ℟.

When we do not support and cooperate with eath other: Lord, have mercy. ℟.

When we neglect prayer: Lord, have mercy. ℟.

Father,
forgive us for having failed to see in the children before us
the sign of your faithfulness and of your presence.
Forgive our impatience, our unwillingness to wait,
our lack of sensitivity and alertness.
Forgive our failure to love and to share.
We make our prayer through Christ Jesus our Lord.

℟. Amen.

FINAL PRAYER AND BLESSING

Lord,
come to us in the community of our Christian school;
may your presence be the deep love in which we grow together,
and the peace that overcomes all obstacles, all conflict.
Make us wakeful as we wait to welcome Christ your Son
into every moment of our lives.
We make our prayer in his name, Jesus Christ our Lord.

℟. Amen.

May the love of the Lord Jesus draw us to himself.

℟. Amen.

May the power of the Lord Jesus strengthen us in his service.

℟. Amen.

May the joy of the Lord Jesus fill our hearts.

℟. Amen.

And may the blessing of almighty God,
the Father, Son and Holy Spirit,
come to us and stay with us always.

℟. Amen.

Go in peace to love and serve the Lord.

℟. Thanks be to God.

CONCLUDING SONG

'Come Lord Jesus, come' FH Vol.1, no.44

The Time of Sickness is a Time of Grace

(for the sick, for general use)

ENTRANCE SONG

'The Lord's my shepherd' PTL, no.115

If those taking part are unable to sing, recorded music can be played; excerpts from the Messiah, the St Matthew Passion, Variations on a Theme by Thomas Tallis (Vaughan-Williams), last movement of the Pastoral Symphony (Beethoven), might be suitable.

GREETING

May the peace of Christ be with you.

INTRODUCTION

My dear friends, when Jesus came to preach repentance, he was bringing us good news, for he was proclaiming to us God's love and mercy. Again and again God comes to our help so that we may turn to him and live our lives entirely in his service. Penance is his gift, a gift we should accept with gratitude. Keeping this in mind, let us open our hearts to God with great simplicity and humility and ask to be reconciled with him as we now forgive each other.

PRAYER

Lord our God,
source of all goodness and mercy,
we come together as your family
to ask your forgiveness
and the forgiveness of each other.
Give us true sorrow for our sins
and loving trust in your compassion
so that we may acknowledge our sins
with sincere hearts.
Through this celebration
restore us to fuller union with yourself
and with our neighbour
so that we may serve you with greater generosity.
We ask this through Christ our Lord.

℟. Amen.

READINGS

Many people enjoy good health and other blessings and accept them as a matter of course, with no sense of gratitude. In time of sickness we discover that all these are great gifts, and that without them we easily lose heart. God allows us to experience suffering in order to test our faith. What is more, if we see our suffering as a share in Christ's suffering, it can be of great value both to ourselves and to the Church. The time of sickness is not then wasted or meaningless. It is in fact a time of grace if we accept it as God wants us to accept it. This celebration is meant to help us to do so. We shall therefore listen to God's word, examine our conscience, and pray with sincere hearts.

The prayer of faith will save the sick man.

James 5.13-16

Pause for reflection

The Son of Man has authority on earth to forgive sins.

Mark 2.1-12

HOMILY

It is appropriate for the celebrant to speak about sickness, especially the sickness of the spirit ('the spirit is willing, but the flesh is weak'). He should emphasize the power of Jesus and his Church to forgive sins, and the value of suffering shared with others and offered for others.

EXAMINATION OF CONSCIENCE

In preparing an examination of conscience for a group of sick people we must try to be aware of their particular difficulties – pain, anger, frustration, fear, loneliness; these are often signs of sickness rather than sinfulness. The examination should aim to encourage rather than to probe. The following questions may be helpful.

Do I fight against God and blame him for my sickness?

Am I grateful for the many blessings I have received during my life?

Do I try to see my sickness as a share in Christ's suffering, and as of value for the conquest of sin in myself and in the world?

Do I pray for greater faith and understanding?

Do I accept that it may be hard for me to pray?

In my loneliness do I try to understand Christ's cry from the cross, 'My God, my God, why have you forsaken me?'

Do I help those who are suffering with me to be happy?

Do I accept what others are doing for me? Do I try to make their task easier?

ACT OF REPENTANCE

I confess to almighty God . . .

Lord our God, we bear the name of your Son and call you Father. We are sorry for our sins against you and against our brothers and sisters.

℟. Give us true repentance and sincere love for you and for our neighbour.

Lord Jesus Christ, you redeemed us by your passion and cross and gave us an example of patience and love. We are sorry for our sins against you, and especially for failing to serve you and our brothers and sisters.

℟. Give us true repentance and sincere love for you and for our neighbour.

Holy Spirit, Lord, you speak to us in the Church and in our conscience and inspire within us the desire to do good. We are sorry for our sins against you, and especially for our obstinate refusal to obey you.

℟. Give us true repentance and sincere love for you and for our neighbour.

Let us ask God our Father to forgive us and to free us from evil:

Our Father . . .

BLESSING

May the God of peace
fill your hearts with every blessing.
May he sustain you
with his gifts of hope and consolation,
help you to offer your lives in his service,
and bring you safely to eternal glory.

May almighty God,
the Father, and the Son, and the Holy Spirit,
grant you all that is good.

℟. Amen.

CONCLUDING SONG

'Where love and loving kindness dwell' PTL, no.188

Through Death to Life

(for the sick, for general use)

ENTRANCE SONG

'I am the bread of life' FH Vol.2, no.57

GREETING

May the peace and the comfort of Jesus Christ be with you all.

INTRODUCTION

We are here today, both the healthy and the sick, so that we might all be made whole by the power of Jesus Christ, who suffered and died so as to rise to the fulness of life. Without faith in resurrection there is no hope. Without suffering and death there is no resurrection. In this service of penance we ask forgiveness for our sins and we ask also that our sufferings may make us more complete human beings both in this world and in the next.

FIRST READING

The reading might be introduced with music, for example, the second movement from Mozart's Clarinet Quintet (Music for Pleasure: CFP 121). Since it is a long reading it can be shared between several voices and could even be dramatised slightly by having someone in the centre of the readers representing Job. As each disaster is reported he bows down and eventually sinks to his knees. Before he speaks he lifts his head and holds out his arms in an attitude of worship. Over the end of the reading fade in the music again.

Job 1.1-22

SECOND READING

That was only the beginning of the story of Job. As with so many stories it has a happy ending with all Job's fortunes being restored. Happy endings for us are in the long run more certain, but they are more difficult to reach. They are more certain because they are founded on the continuing love of the living Jesus. They are more difficult to reach because the love of Jesus leads us through death itself.

1 Corinthians 13.1-13

GOSPEL READING

Through love, suffering and death we reach the kingdom of heaven. And in that kingdom what sort of happiness awaits us?

Matthew 5.1-12

HOMILY OUTLINE

* The happiness of the kingdom is the happiness which completes our lives.

* It is no use asking, 'Why is there suffering? Why is there death?' There could be no love (and no kingdom) if there were no suffering and death.

* If our actions could not harm others, if there was no purpose in our concern for others, if there could never be a separation as final as death, then there could be no love, no completion, no happiness.

* Jesus was raised to glory through his suffering and death.

EXAMINATION OF CONSCIENCE

Let us now examine our lives in the light of this gospel, remembering those times we have tried to evade the demands of love and been angry or hopeless under the weight of suffering.

Let us think particularly of the opportunities suffering has provided us with for showing our love, opportunities which we may sometimes have rejected.

Let us think about the life and the death of Jesus and the times we have failed to join our sufferings with his as a loving offering to the world.

ACT OF REPENTANCE

Father almighty and ever loving God,
it was your wisdom that made the world;
it is your love that leads us to the joys of your kingdom.
Forgive us our lack of faith and have mercy on us in our suffering.

For the times we have been angry and refused to accept your will: in your mercy,

℟. Forgive us Lord.

For the times we have failed to appreciate the sufferings of others: in your mercy,

℟. Forgive us Lord.

For the times we have refused to help: in your mercy,

℟. Forgive us Lord.

For the times we have failed to love: in your mercy,

℟. Forgive us Lord.

Now let us say together the Lord's prayer.

Our Father . . .

BLESSING

The celebrant may go to each of the sick and bless them individually.

May Jesus Christ be with you in your suffering,
and may you be brought to loving health in his kingdom.
In the name of the Father,
and of the Son,
and of the Holy Spirit.

℟. Amen.

May the peace and the love of Christ
be with you and stay with you for ever.

℟. Amen.

FINAL SONG

'I am the bread of life' FH Vol.2, no.57

You are Not Forgotten

(for the sick, for general use)

ENTRANCE SONG

'Walk with me, O my Lord' FH Vol.2, no.2

GREETING

Jesus said, 'I have come that they might have life to the full.' May he turn your sufferings into joy, giving you peace and forgiveness.

INTRODUCTION

When we are ill, we may feel rejected by God, disabled from a real following of Christ, shut away from the community of the Church. We are here today to gain encouragement from the realisation that we are not alone, that we have a special place in God's design and in Christ's love, and that God is always forgiving.

FIRST READING

Christ rose to glory through suffering. If we wish to rise with him and share his glory, we must expect to share his cross. But even on the cross we can be sure that nothing can separate us from the love of God. We are not forgotten.

Romans 8.28-39

Pause for reflection

Psalm 15(16).8,9,11

℟. I am the resurrection and the life, says the Lord.

GOSPEL READING

The sick man had been waiting at the pool for 38 years. Forgiveness – real health – is never impossible.

John 5.1-9

HOMILY OUTLINE

* By their prayers and sufferings, the sick have a special role in the mission of the Church.

* Acceptance of God's will does not mean passive resignation: Jesus made the sick whole again.

* The healing miracles of Jesus are signs of the coming of God's kingdom: he can heal us still in the way he sees best.

* The core of the gospel message is that death is the way to life, sorrow the way to joy: they are the stuff out of which life and joy are created.

PRAYER

Jesus experienced to the full our human situation, our strength and our weakness. Let us pray to his Father and ours for courage to accept our weakness, and for the strength he wants to give us.

Pause for silent prayer

God our Father,
when we acknowledge our weakness
you are able to do great things in us.
Help us to accept ourselves as we are, loved by you.
May we turn to you in perfect trust,
for forgiveness and healing.

Through Jesus Christ our Lord.

℟. Amen.

EXAMINATION OF CONSCIENCE

Illness – mental or physical – causes particular tensions, problems, frustrations. We are conscious of a weakness which often makes it impossible for us to be as patient, kind and grateful as we should like. Especially if we have to face a long illness, we need to come to terms with all these difficulties, to accept them as the conditions in which we have to follow Jesus. We need to turn to God with a deep confidence that he is our loving Father, and that we have a special part in the work of the Church.

ACT OF REPENTANCE

If we have imagined that our illness was a sign that God no longer loved us: Father, forgive us.

℟. Father, forgive us.

If we have felt that our lives were without any purpose: Father, forgive us. ℟.

If we have given way to impatience, or been exacting and difficult with those who look after us: Father, forgive us. ℟.

If we have been upset about our failures in patience, kindness, gratitude, trust, because they spoiled our picture of ourselves: Father, forgive us. ℟.

If we have let our own illness or pain loom so large that we have had no sympathy to spare for other people: Father, forgive us. ℟.

FINAL PRAYER

God our Father,
in your plan for the world
life comes out of death, joy out of sorrow.
You have called us to share in your Son's suffering;
may we experience the joy of his resurrection.
We make our prayer through him,
and by the power of the Holy Spirit.

℟. Amen.

BLESSING

May God our Father give you the assurance of his love.

℟. Amen.

May our Lord Jesus Christ heal you in the way that is best for you.

℟. Amen.

May the Holy Spirit fill you with his gifts of love, joy, peace and patience.

℟. Amen.

And may the blessing of almighty God,
the Father, the Son and the Holy Spirit,
come down on you and remain with you always.

℟. Amen.

CONCLUDING SONG

'Peace, perfect peace' FH Vol.1, no.2

Form of Examination of Conscience

(for general use, to be adapted for particular groups)

We should first ask ourselves these questions:

* What is our attitude to the sacrament of penance? Do we sincerely want to be set free from sin, to turn again to God, to begin a new life, and to enter into a deeper friendship with God? Or do we look on it as a burden, to be undertaken as seldom as possible?

* Have we forgotten to mention, or deliberately concealed, any grave sins in past celebrations of the sacrament?

* Have we done the penance we were given? Did we make reparation for any injury to others? Have we tried to put into practice our resolution to lead a life more in keeping with the Gospel?

We should now examine our lives in the light of God's word.

The Lord says: 'You shall love the Lord your God with your whole heart.'

* Are our hearts set on God, so that we really love him above all things and are faithful to his commandments, as children love their father? Or are we more concerned about the things of this world? Have we a right intention in what we do?

* God spoke to us in his Son. Is our faith in God firm and secure? Are we wholehearted in accepting the Church's teaching? Have we been careful to grow in our understanding of the faith, to hear God's word, to listen to instructions on the faith, to avoid dangers to faith? Have we been always strong and fearless in professing our faith in God and the Church? Have we been willing to be known as Christians in private and public life?

* Have we prayed morning and evening? When we pray, do we really raise mind and heart to God or is it a matter of words only? Do we offer God our difficulties, our joys, and our sorrows? Do we turn to God in times of temptation?

* Have we love and reverence for God's name? Have we offended him in blasphemy, swearing falsely, or taking his name in vain? Have we shown disrespect for the Blessed Virgin Mary and the saints?

* Do we keep Sundays and feast days holy by taking a full part, with attention and devotion, in the liturgy, and especially in the Mass? Have we fulfilled the precept of annual confession and of communion during the Easter season?

* Are there false gods that we worship by giving them greater attention and deeper trust than we give to God: money, superstition, spiritism, or other occult practices?

The Lord says: 'Love one another as I have loved you.'

* Have we a genuine love for our neighbours? Or do we use them for our own ends, or do to them what we would not want done to ourselves? Have we given grave scandal by our words or actions?

* In our family life, have we contributed to the well-being and happiness of the rest of the family by patience and genuine love? Have we been obedient to parents, showing them proper respect and giving them help in their spiritual and material needs? Have we been careful to give a Christian upbringing to our children, and to help them by good example and by exercising sound authority as parents? Have we been faithful to husband (wife) in our hearts and in our relations with others?

* Do we share our possessions with the less fortunate? Do we do our best to help the victims of oppression, misfortune, and poverty? Or do we look down on our neighbour, especially the poor, the sick, the elderly, strangers, and people of other races?

* Do our lives reflect the mission we received in confirmation? Do we share in the apostolic and charitable works of the Church and in the life of our parish? Have we helped to meet the needs of the Church and of the world and prayed for them: for unity in the Church, for the spread of the gospel among nations, for peace and justice, etc.?

* Are we concerned for the good and prosperity of the human community in which we live, or do we spend our lives caring only for ourselves? Do we share to the best of our ability in the work of promoting justice, morality, harmony, and love in human relations? Have we done our duty as citizens? Have we paid our taxes?

* In our work or profession are we just, hard-working, honest, serving society out of love for others? Have we paid fair wages to our employees? Have we been faithful to our promises and contracts?

* Have we obeyed legitimate authority and given it due respect?

* If we are in positions of responsibility or authority, do we use this for our own advantage or for the good of others, in a spirit of service?

* Have we been truthful and fair, or have we injured others by deceit, calumny, detraction, rash judgment, or violation of a secret?

* Have we done violence to others by damage to life or limb, reputation, honour, or material possessions? Have we involved them in loss? Have we been responsible for advising an abortion or procuring one? Have we kept up hatred for others? Are we estranged from others through quarrels, enmity, insults, anger? Have we been guilty of refusing to testify to the innocence of another because of selfishness?

* Have we stolen the property of others? Have we desired it unjustly and inordinately? Have we damaged it? Have we made restitution of other people's property and made good their loss?

* If we have been injured, have we been ready to make peace for the love of Christ and to forgive, or do we harbour hatred and the desire for revenge?

Christ our Lord says: 'Be perfect as your Father is perfect.'

* Where are our lives really leading us? Is the hope of eternal life our inspiration? Have we tried to grow in the life of the Spirit through prayer, reading the word of God and meditating on it, receiving the sacraments, self-denial? Have we been anxious to control our vices, our bad inclinations and passions, eg, envy, love of food and drink? Have we been proud and boastful, thinking ourselves better in the sight of God and despising others as less important than ourselves? Have we imposed our own wills on others, without respecting their freedom and rights?

* What use have we made of time, of health and strength, of the gifts God has given us to be used like the talents in the Gospel? Do we use them to become more perfect every day? Or have we been lazy and too much given to leisure?

* Have we been patient in accepting the sorrows and disappointments of life? How have we performed mortification so as to 'fill up what is lacking in the sufferings of Christ'? Have we kept the precept of fasting and abstinence?

* Have we kept senses and body pure and chaste as a temple of the Holy Spirit consecrated for resurrection and glory, and as a sign of

God's faithful love for men and women, a sign that is seen most perfectly in the sacrament of matrimony? Have we dishonoured our bodies by fornication, impurity, unworthy conversation or thoughts, evil desires or actions? Have we given in to sensuality? Have we indulged in reading, conversation, shows and entertainments that offend against Christian and human decency? Have we encouraged others to sin by our own failure to maintain these standards? Have we been faithful to the moral law in our married life?

* Have we gone against our consciences out of fear or hypocrisy?

* Have we always tried to act in the true freedom of the sons of God according to the law of the Spirit, or are we slaves of forces within us?

Bibliography

A short bibliography of useful reference and source books is given.

Jerusalem Bible (Darton, Longman and Todd)
RSV Bible (Nelson)
New English Bible (O.U.P.)
The Psalms. A New Translation. (Fontana)
Good News for Modern Man (Fontana)
Winding Quest (Old Testament) Alan Dale (O.U.P.)
New World (New Testament) Alan Dale (O.U.P.)
A Child's Bible – Old Testament (Piccolo)
A Child's Bible – New Testament (Piccolo)
A Children's Lectionary (Paulist Press)
A Christian's Prayer Book ed. Peter Coughlan and others (Chapman)
A Liturgy of Life David Konstant (Mayhew-McCrimmon)
A Penitent's Prayer Book ed. David Konstant (Mayhew-McCrimmon)
Prayers of Life Quoist (Gill)
Stay With Us Chagneau (Newman)
You Call Us Together Griolet (Paulist Press)
Your Word is Near Oosterhuis (Paulist Press)
Open Your Hearts Oosterhuis (Sheed & Ward)
Words for Worship Campling & Davis (Arnold)
Word Alive ed. Banyard (Belton Books)
Worship and Wonder ed. Jones (Galliard)
It's Me, O Lord Hollings & Gullick (Mayhew-McCrimmon)
Day by Day Purton (Blackwell)
Epilogues and Prayers Barclay (S.C.M.)
Contemporary Prayers ed. Micklem (S.C.M.)
More Contemporary Prayers ed. Micklem (S.C.M.)
Listen to Love ed. Savary (Regina Press)
The Heart has its Seasons ed. Savary (Regina Press)
A Time for Salvation ed. Savary (Regina Press)
Horizons of Hope ed. Blue & Savary (St Mary's College Press)
Faces of Freedom ed. Blue & Savary (St Mary's College Press)
Readings Thompson (C.U.P.)
The Ministry of Reconciliation: A commentary on the order of penance 1974 J. D. Crichton (Chapman)
Penance: Introduction to the New Rite (C.T.S.)
Penance: Commentaries on the New Rite (C.T.S.)
Penance: A Pastoral Presentation (C.T.S.)